HOW TO GET THINGS
REALLY FLAT

ANDREW MARTIN

HOW
TO
GET
THINGS
REALLY FLAT

Enlightenment for Every Man
on Ironing, Vacuuming and
Other Household Arts

THE EXPERIMENT
NEW YORK

The Experiment, LLC
260 Fifth Avenue
New York, NY 10001-6425
www.theexperimentpublishing.com

This U.S. edition, emended from the original UK edition,
is published by arrangement with Short Books.

Library of Congress Control Number: 2009925217
ISBN 978-1-61519-002-7

Cover design and photograph by Michael Fusco Design | michaelfuscodesign.com
Design by Pauline Neuwirth, Neuwirth & Associates, Inc.

Manufactured in the United States of America

First printing September 2009

10 9 8 7 6 5 4 3 2 1

This book is dedicated to, but not intended for, Lisa

CONTENTS

HOW TO GET THINGS
REALLY FLAT

PREFACE
TO THE AMERICAN EDITION

It's very satisfying to write those words, but it seems strange to be doing so in connection with this subject. As I survey my notes for this book, scribblings such as "Vacuuming—basic facts" and "Get more on dusting" seem bizarre. That I should have accumulated a pile of paper about six inches thick on the various disciplines* of housework seems odder still.

The belief that men are just not supposed to know about housework is particularly strong in the North of England, which is where I grew up. During my childhood, the region was still the industrial heart of Britain, as it had been since the early nineteenth century. A friend of mine recently said to me, "There's a great arrogance about northerners, isn't there? That's because they come from the world's first industrialized region—it's there in

---

*That's putting it rather grandly. A man can learn to do almost any aspect of housework properly in five minutes if he pays attention—and, what is more, he will never forget.

their DNA." Personally, I think this empowering inner knowledge has been washed away on a tide of cappuccino, Frappuccino, drizzled pesto, and other manifestations of the service economy that have replaced industrial production. I grew up in York, a popular tourist destination for American visitors. The industry of York was rather reprehensibly pretty: railways and chocolate. But still, the medieval city walls, which today gleam white for the benefit of tourists, were once black from locomotive smoke, and I wasn't allowed to go near them if wearing a smart coat. At five o'clock the men were released from the railway carriage works—three thousand blokes riding wobbly bikes ten abreast down the road. At night I went asleep to sound of (or was kept awake by) the ghostly clanking of wagons being shunted. Most days, the air of the city was also permeated with the soft, deliquescing smell of roasted cacao beans from the two great chocolate factories. Today the carriage works is closed, and there's a huge, embarrassing empty space around the station where the freight-marshaling yards used to be. One chocolate factory is about to be turned into a hotel; the other survives, but in reduced circumstances, and you have to be standing in the right place at the right time to get the chocolate smell.

My grandfather was an engineer in one of the chocolate factories, and my father and mother both worked for British Rail. But then, when I was nine, my mother died, and my grief was compounded by social disorientation.

Who would do the housework? The idea that my father might do it seemed a very radical piece of lateral thinking indeed. For one thing, this would require him to be at large in the kitchen and in the house generally, yet northern men at that time were hardly ever seen by my young eyes. They were remote, haggard figures. You'd see them going to work and coming back from work. Otherwise they were in bed or in the pub.

In Northern England, the deal was this: the man went to work in a factory or similar; the wife (and he often *would* employ the definite article when speaking of his spouse) got to stay at home, in return for which privilege she would do the housework—and I do mean all of it. This division of labor was at its height in Edwardian times, when any working-class man who helped about the house would be an object of abuse: he was a "dolly-mop" or simply a "nancy." The logic was that if this betrayer of the male sex was doing housework, then his wife must be destined for the factory. In my boyhood, the man who did housework was still a freak, even if he had no wife to *send* to the factory, and I—a self-conscious youth—became particularly aware of my father's anomalous position during Sunday lunchtimes when, just as the women's labors were at their most frenetic in the cooking of the big meal, the men strolled off to the pub. But *my* dad stayed at home, filling the kitchen with steam as he boiled the vegetables to death. I'd watch the other fathers going past the kitchen window, passing out Hamlet cigars and laughing in anticipation of a couple of pints and a game of dominoes, and I'd say, "Don't you want to go to the pub, Dad?"

"No, I don't, now will you pass me the gravy mix?"

Why didn't he want to go to the pub? It struck me that he was rather suspiciously keen on doing the housework. He was taking to it rather too well.

Then again, had he not also played professional football as a young man when he'd turned out (admittedly only once) for York City, who were then not quite as negligible a footballing force as they subsequently became? Was he not a faster runner than me, as proved every year on Blackpool beach? Had he not—during a trip to London—shoved a big man halfway down an escalator when he'd ignored a polite "Excuse me," repeated three times? Also, his housework specialty was ironing (he would carefully lay a thin piece of damp muslin over my school trousers and press down hard with the iron to give razor creases), and this skill, I knew, he had learned in the army.

"I always had an iron under my control in the billet," my dad once told me, "and I would do the ironing for the blokes who couldn't do it themselves. I'd always iron the cook's uniform, and he paid me back with toast and tea."

My dad was no dolly-mop, and as I got older, I stopped worrying so much about it. Nevertheless, I felt it would be best for him—safer for his mental health, as it were—to minimize the amount of time he spent wearing an apron (because he would put one on for the heavier kitchen jobs). So I began to help him with the housework, in which activity lie the roots of this book.

In the writing of it, I came up against the old prejudice—which has faded but certainly not gone away with the elimination of the industry that prompted it—and a few new ones. For example, when I told my two sons, ages eleven and thirteen, that I was writing a book on housework for men, one of them said, "Dad, aren't you going to look a bit gay doing that?"

"I'm not bothered about that," I said, and I might have quoted at him the domestic watchword of the late Quentin Crisp, than whom it would be difficult to be more gay: "There is no need to do any housework. After the first four years the dirt doesn't get any worse."

My other son was equally discouraging, but in a different way. "Isn't your book a bit sexist," he fretted, "because it assumes men don't do any housework?"

Well, I like to think that between them the boys encompassed the widest possible range of knee-jerk prejudice, and I feel that I ought to make an opening statement in response. This book is billed as "a man's guide," but that man could of course be one of two sharing a household, or "he" could be a woman. The book is aimed at the designated slob, the Walter Matthau of *The Odd Couple* rather than the Jack Lemmon. It is for the person who does not know, or care, what day the garbagemen come, or where the bathroom cleaner is kept, or what starch is.

If you said the word *limescale* to this person, it would trigger nothing in their brain. These people have to ask the gasman where the gas meter is rather than the other way around, and they think that a crevice attachment is something used in rock climbing. (In fact, it's the thinnest—and, as I hope to demonstrate, by far the most interesting and "fun"—attachment of the vacuum cleaner.)

Usually, however, the person in that Walter Matthau role will be a man, and usually he will be living with a woman. I have asked my male friends what they do about the house, and only one gave an expansive answer: "Every morning, I make the children's breakfasts, wash up the things from the night before, and generally reduce the place to the state of a show house . . ." he began, but his two children, climbing a tree some feet away, kept butting in, "Come off it, Dad!" "When do you do that?" "*We've* never seen you."

Most of the men had something to say, like a defendant offering some feeble mitigation before sentence is passed: "I always wash up after the evening meal. . . . I do most of the cooking at the weekends." But in the main, their answers were characterised by an extreme brevity:

"Help when I can."

"Emptying the dishwasher—that's my job."

"Depends if I'm around," one man airily responded.

Then again, the wives or partners of these men would be able to answer in fewer words still, because they do "everything else."

If women don't do most of the housework, then why

are cleaning products advertised on weekday mornings, and not during the halftimes of football games? Why is it a woman who is shown looking perplexed during an advertisement as the voiceover intones, "You want to remove tough stains from colored clothes but you're worried about the color coming out?" or pleased at the news that "Harpic three-in-one works twenty-four seven." And if women don't do most of the housework, why are 99 percent of all books written about housework written by women?

At the time of writing, the number of British women who describe their main occupation as that of "looking after the family or the house" is 2.1 million, whereas the number of British men who so describe themselves is 207,000. In 1993, the corresponding figures were 2.7 million and 108,000, respectively. Gender roles are dissolving under the influence of decreasing job security, higher divorce rates, and—I suppose—feminist persuasion, but they are dissolving very slowly.

In 2005, Dr. Caroline Gatrell's book *Hard Labour: The Sociology of Parenthood* was first published. It contains the results of Dr. Gatrell's interviews conducted with twenty highly qualified British couples with children. In each case the woman was in employment. "As far as the domestic division of labour was concerned," Dr. Gatrell writes, "the situation for mothers was depressingly familiar, and echoed the findings of key writers on domestic labour during the previous two decades in that women bore the brunt of domestic work, no matter how many hours of paid work they undertook."

I have always believed the situation to be the same in America. I have never seen Homer Simpson doing the washing up, just as I have never seen Clint Eastwood vacuuming.* According to a study released in 2008 by the Institute for Social Research at the University of Michigan, Ann Arbor, American women without children do, on average, ten hours of housework a week before marriage and seventeen hours after marriage; men without children do eight hours before marriage and seven hours afterward. Married women with more than three children do an average of twenty-eight hours of housework a week, while married men with more than three children do about ten hours.

Many men of today would call themselves feminists, but how many of them regularly put in a load of washing? I am in favor of a basic equity in housework: do as you would be done by; leave this toilet in the state you would expect to find it, as the notices have it in the worst sorts of public lavatories. But I am not a feminist writer, or a new man, or a househusband. To my mind, the fact that your wife might want you to do more of the housework is only one good reason for doing it, and I hope it will become evident that *How to Get Things Really Flat* is not about how to help your wife so much as it is about how to help yourself.

---

* If he were going to do it at all, then he would have done it in his latest film, *Gran Torino.* In this, he plays a widower with a large suburban house to look after, but he is only seen doing the "manly" jobs, such as arranging the tools in his garage or mowing the lawn, or threatening to shoot people who step on that lawn.

1

Why Do Housework?*

Sorry to insist upon this point, as it may seem rather maudlin and Dickensian of me, but my mother did die when I was quite a young boy, whereupon York City council supplied my father with a "home help" to assist with the housework. She was called, somehow aptly, Mrs. Buffard, and she came on Monday, Wednesday, and Friday mornings. She was a very jolly woman and I liked having her around, but what I particularly liked was the state of the house just after she'd left it. It was clean and tidy, and seemed sunnier. There was mysterious, rather beautiful midnight-blue stuff in the toilets

---

* It may be enough, for a certain type of man, if I mention that the San Francisco-based psychologist Joshua Coleman, author of *The Lazy Husband: How to Get Men to Do More Parenting and Housework*, has said that wives are likely to harbor greater feelings of sexual interest in men who participated in housework.

(Harpic,* as I am now able to deduce). I knew that after one flush the blue stuff in the toilet would be gone, and I'd defer peeing to keep it there.

Mrs. Buffard made my bed so neatly that I would try to slide into it without disrupting it, and my aim was to get out of a made bed in the morning. In my bedroom, the window would be left slightly open for the purposes of airing, and my *Whizzer and Chips* and *Beano* comics all looked much more plausible, more *intellectual* somehow, when marshaled into neat piles. I noticed that Mrs. Buffard left the tea towel hanging on the kitchen washing line, and I would marvel at this: I'd never thought of hanging it up like that. *I'd* thought I was doing everybody a favor by folding it up into a square about six inches wide after using it. She would also leave the dishcloth hanging over the two kitchen taps to dry, which I thought was a decorative touch; I didn't realize at the time that this was good hygienic practice, since bacteria thrive on moisture.

When Mrs. Buffard had finished with the house, it was all ready for living in. A clean house was a suitable basis for getting things done. I would try to invite my friends around shortly after she'd left—not quite while she was

---

* Harpic has been making toilet-cleaning liquids, tablets, blocks, wipes, and brushes for the British market since the 1920s. The name is also well known, apparently, in Eastern Europe, Africa, the Middle East, and Latin America, but not in America. In the 1930s and 1940s, an eccentric Briton might be said to be "a bit Harpic," the rationale being as follows: the original blue cleaner was advertised in the 1930s as cleaning "round the bend," meaning the U-bend, and in Britain "round the bend" is slang for mad.

there, because it was slightly shameful to have a home help. It implied helplessness. But my friends, whether through diplomacy or ignorance, would refer to Mrs. Buffard as "your cleaner," just as though we paid for her services, and I wouldn't go out of my way to correct this misapprehension.

I knew that Mrs. Buffard came, in some way, from the government, and it was rather worrying that they—or it—should have thought it necessary to send her. For a year or so after my mother's death, I'd noticed people furtively congratulating my father on keeping the family together, on "keeping the children on," which was alarming and made me think that this decision of his might be reversible. Even with Mrs. Buffard's help, it might all suddenly become too much for him, and he might decide to do whatever was the opposite of keeping us on. Seeing my father in close conversation with another adult, I would sidle up alongside, just in case he was saying, "I've found a very good orphanage for Andrew . . . a very smart uniform, all mod cons, and reasonable visiting hours."

This was partly why I began to do some of the housework myself. I instituted a nightly routine. Coming home from school, I'd wash any dishes left over from breakfast, wipe down what I did not then call "the kitchen surfaces," hang the tea towel over the kitchen line, and leave the dishcloth strung across the taps à la Mrs. Buffard. I'd run over the living room with the Ewbank (carpet sweeper), take the dustpan and brush to the area beneath the canary's cage, shake the hearth rug in the garden (indeed, so vigorously that the backing would repeatedly fall off), and straighten the antimacassars on the chairs. Only then could I sit down and watch children's TV.

I started doing that when I was ten. At age eleven, I duly failed my Eleven Plus* and went to a secondary modern school, which taught practical skills to ready its pupils for careers in the industry that, as it turned out, Mrs. Thatcher would shortly come along and abolish. The boys did a lot of metalwork and woodwork; the girls did cookery and needlework. For one experimental term, these roles were reversed and—in what was probably the most momentous single school lesson I ever attended— a Mrs. Davies taught me how to cook an omelet *and* an apple crumble and custard. (Didn't hang about, that Mrs. Davies.) I should think that I've cooked an average of two omelets a week ever since. Apple crumbles I knock off less often, but it's what you'll have for pudding if you come to dinner here**.

I found a freedom in the kitchen, whether cooking or cleaning. It was a place where you could be with no questions asked. I believe that my father felt the same. We

---

*A test made up of questions beginning "If John has six apples, and Mary has four . . ." that decided your whole fate. If you passed it, you would be educated at a grammar school, which is to say that you would be properly educated. It has now been largely abolished. I have always wanted to append a footnote to the bald statement of my failure in the exam: the fact is that I had a headache and realized too late that I had missed a page.

** Our "pudding" is your "dessert."

were both antisocial, and one thing about housework . . . it gets you out of talking to people. (See chapter 4: Washing Up.) Also, kitchen work, far from being a sort of domestic imprisonment, made me feel free: an independent unit, as the Edwardians used to say. I could "manage"; I could look after myself, and if I could do it in this one house, then I could do it in any other.

As I reached young manhood, some of my male friends "came out"—on school camps, in student digs, and so on—as people who couldn't cook, and I remember the shrill, panicking tone of a friend who said he wouldn't be taking his turn at the cooker in the shared holiday home because he didn't know how. Later, at university, I would note the shamefaced look on my friends' faces as, at the end of term, they loaded a mountain of dirty laundry into Mummy's car. This was completely incompatible with the swaggering persona they presented every day in the junior common room.

Today I often meet men who proudly declare that they never do any housework, while their wives muster strange, forced, curdled smiles in the background. The existence of these men seems to me unreal. They are living on borrowed time, desperately vulnerable and poised for disaster, like those cartoon characters who've run off the edge of a cliff and not realized. But I know they're about to find out at any minute . . . when their wives leave them, I mean. Dr. Gatrell, author of *Hard Labour*, observed in her interviewees that "the domestic division of labour became a serious issue following the birth of the first child," and when I spoke to her she told me that the second time it becomes a big issue is "during divorce proceedings."

But I do not seek to present myself as a domestic paragon. The domestic scenes of my early manhood were pure *Withnail and I* squalor for years on end—a testament to the power of the human immune system. And when I got married in my midthirties, the familiar discrepancy appeared between me and my wife.

Here was a woman—a journalist—who had once been late for an important meeting with her editor (he was threatening to sack her), having been unable to leave the house without first making her bed and tidying the kitchen, even though she was well aware of having overslept. (She did get sacked, but a bit later on.) My wife has very high standards when it comes to washing up, tidying up, and bathroom and kitchen cleanliness. She's also very keen—much to my secret satisfaction—that the house should look right, and there's an element of skillful stage dressing to her tidying up. Her attitude toward housework is based on aesthetics rather than an obsessive-compulsive desire to disinfect everything in sight. But while I did more housework than the average man, we would still have rows about it, especially after the boys were born. Or the arguments wouldn't be about housework to begin with, but they'd soon get there. "This week," my wife would say, "I've done the shopping, put in three loads of laundry, spent five hours ironing all the clothes including yours, made breakfast every day and the evening meal most days; I've vacuumed twice, mopped the kitchen floor . . ."

For a man, there is no "Yes, but . . ." after that. You've lost the argument, however reasonable the point you might have been trying to make in the first place.

I turned over the problem in my mind for a long time. What were the known parameters? My wife did about four times more housework than I did. It was obviously getting her down, since she also did—and does—work a full-time job. More important, it was getting me down, too. The feelings of guilt; the lack of bargaining power; the sense of being a spare part, of aspiring to an anachronistic male role . . . What to do? The answer came to me one Sunday evening.

That was my evening for going off to the pub for a couple of pints. It was also the evening that my wife did the ironing, usually in front of the costume drama on TV, and we would coincide somewhere near the front door shortly after the children had gone to bed: she would be approaching the living room, her upper body entirely hidden behind a stack of ironing; I would be rounding up the sports sections of the papers in order to read them in the pub.

On this particular Sunday, as I opened the door, and called out my habitual, "See you a bit later, then," I noticed a certain lack of enthusiasm in her habitual "Have a nice time." As I wandered over to the pub, I thought this over:

perhaps it was just that her voice had been muffled by all the laundry she'd been carrying as she spoke—it *had* toppled over onto her face somewhat—or perhaps it was just the strain of lifting it.

I had a particularly meditative couple of pints in the pub, and I hardly touched those sports sections. On returning to the house, I entered the living room, took off my coat, sat down, and said, "I've something to tell you."

"Yes?" she said, a little alarmed as she aligned the creases on a pair of my trousers.

"I've decided to take over the ironing," I said.

For a while she just eyed me suspiciously.

"All of it?" she said.

"All of it."

"Good," she said.

But she seemed a bit shell-shocked.

"I'm not letting you do the napkins," she said, after a while.

I explained to her that she was obviously like those institutionalized prisoners who wouldn't take their opportunity for freedom when it came.

"No, it's not that," she said. "I just don't trust you with the napkins."

"Don't you want me to do the ironing?"

"Of course I do . . . of *course* I do."

It was all very low key, as important pivotal moments often are. We just both knew it was the right thing, and there was nothing further to say.

It was one of the best decisions I've ever made, and I commend it to my readers. If anything, I go to the pub more now than I used to, feeling guilt free and often leaving a pile of freshly if not particularly well-pressed clothes in my wake. My wife's "Have a nice time" has regained its merry ring, not least because I have branched out from ironing to doing the laundry, or "washing the clothes," as I like to call it. This happened because the iron, I discovered, was kept near the washing machine, and when I squared up to this contraption I saw it was not quite so complicated as I had always suspected. I have developed a basic method of washing the clothes, which leaves them definitely cleaner than they were before (I will put it no higher than that), and which I will outline in the next chapter.

Mindful of the lightened mood in the house that resulted from my work in these areas, I rediscovered my boyhood enjoyment of vacuuming, becoming—if I do say so myself—something of a specialist with the aforementioned crevice attachment (See chapter 5: Vacuuming). I now quite often clean the bath and have even dabbled in toilet cleaning. For several weeks—until my wife reclaimed the job on the grounds that "there's never any food in the house"—I did the family shopping, and for a couple of those weeks, I think I did the job exceptionally well. (There *was* food in the house—it just wasn't necessarily food that anybody wanted to eat.)

It would be hubristic, and possibly wrong, to say that we argue less. To some extent we just argue about different, more worthwhile things, and, because the moral imbalance has been partly redressed, I win more often than I used to.

2

Doing a Wash

WHY WASH THE CLOTHES?

You should do the washing because you can, because it is so easy compared with how things were. A hundred years ago, laundry took up the entirety of Monday at the very least. It was considered decadent to leave it until late in the week, and also impractical. An old bit of Yorkshire philosophy runs: "Them as wash on Monday have the whole week to dry." It was still labor intensive enough in the 1960s when, as a boy, I would watch my mother do the job.

The washing machine was an ugly, jaundiced-looking thing perched on high wheels and bearing the grandiose legend "Made for English Electric by ACME" (or was it the other way around?). It was not plumbed in like the modern machines, but had to be dragged over toward the kitchen sink, where it was filled from a rubber hose connected to the faucet. As the machine throbbed away, boiling the water, the kitchen filled with steam, and everything conspired to make a melancholy mood: the feeble chirpiness of Jimmy Young on Radio Two; the rain falling outside and all but falling inside as well; the fact that it was Monday; the fact that because the washing was going on, nothing else could be going on, therefore lunch was likely to be canned spaghetti on toast.

When the clothes had been washed . . . well, that was only the beginning. My mother would haul them out of the machine with wooden tongs, which had been bleached to the color of bone by immersion in boiling water, and then push them up the little steel slope toward the mangle that was attached to the machine. Sometimes I was allowed to help feed the clothes into the mangle. I liked doing that. The mangle rollers were omnivorous and always hungry. You only needed to snag the tiniest corner of a garment between the rollers for it to be eagerly taken up. But I knew it was dangerous work, and my mother stood over me as I did it. The mangle, like bleach, was one of the dangerous emanations of housework. I knew of a boy who'd somehow gotten his arm caught in the mangle, so that the skin around his elbow was all crumpled up. (At least, he *said* he'd got his arm caught in the mangle, but it occurs to me all these years later that this might just have been his way of glamorizing a birthmark or skin condition.)

The traumatized, mangle-flattened clothes were then carried directly out to dry on the line—until about 1970, when we acquired a spin-dryer. With this ferocious, dwarfish machine, you clamped down the lid and then placed a bucket by the outlet pipe to catch the water that would be spun out of the clothes. The water didn't come immediately, and waiting for it was like waiting for somebody to be sick. You then had to whip the bucket away, because as it reached the climax of its spinning, the dryer would have an epileptic fit, juddering about the room with such terrifying violence that as a child I would not be alone in the kitchen with it. (When my mother died and my father took over washing the clothes, he would quite often quell the thing by sitting on it, sometimes while reading the paper.)

Without a spin-dryer, drying the clothes was easier said than done in rainy Yorkshire. On a wet day, some clothes would be placed on the wooden drying rack, which could be raised or lowered on a pulley from the kitchen ceiling like a flat in the theater. Alternately, the clothes were loaded onto our two wooden clotheshorses and placed around the gas miser.

On a fine day, it was my job to take the wet laundry into the back garden and hang it on the line. Having finished the job, I would proudly raise the level of the clothesline with a wooden clothes prop, like a soldier raising a flag after victory in a battle (though of course the ironing was still to be done).

Today, washing machines are plumbed in, so you don't have to haul them over to the sink before using them. They are operated at the flick of a couple of buttons, and the spin cycle does the job of the old, manic spin-dryers. You can fill the machine, select from various settings, and switch it on while waiting for your tea to steep. So it does seem churlish not to put in a load occasionally, especially since you're only going to be doing a wash, and not doing "the laundry."

WHAT IS THE DIFFERENCE BETWEEN DOING A WASH AND DOING THE LAUNDRY?

Some people—and by "people" I mean "women"—are really into doing "the laundry," which is not so much a single job as a regime that can eat up most of the week. It is as if they are determined that the invention of the computerized washing machine should not bring them any significant saving of time. Let's look at the difference between doing the laundry and doing a wash.

The standard books on home care, the ones written by and for women, will have around twenty pages on laundry/washing before coming to the point at which the washing machine door is opened to receive the dirty clothes. Here are some of the recommended preliminaries that you may—but probably won't want to—adopt.

Instead of making do with one laundry basket for the whole family, you might acquire about half a dozen of them, which you will label for the purpose of sorting your laundry into cotton whites, cotton coloreds, man-made fibers, woolens, and so on. Next, rather than just shoving the clothes into the machine while thinking about something else, you will scrutinize all of the clothes in these baskets, deliberately seeking out the kinds of stubborn stains most likely to cause you a headache, and you will then have a go at "spot cleaning" these with a localized application of detergent or some proprietary spot cleaner custom-made for that particular stain. Or you might think it best to thoroughly wash some or all the clothes by hand before entrusting them to the washing machine, reasoning that the way to make sure the clothes are clean at the end of the washing machine cycle is to make sure they are clean at the *start* of it.

You will then put the clothes into the machine individually, checking the shirts for cufflinks and the children's clothes for badges and other accoutrements. You will check inside all of the pockets, and not just in the hope of stealing some money belonging to another family member, but to search for anything that might affect the wash or be affected by it. Fancy buttons you will naturally want to remove with scissors before stitching them back on later.

Then, instead of bunging in a cupful of Persil,* pressing

---

* Every British man knows that Persil "washes whiter" even if the matter is of purely academic interest to him.

the On button and shouting "Right, I've done the wash! I'm off to the pub now!" you will select just the right detergent for that particular wash, whether biological (containing enzymes for an added boost), nonbiological, liquid, or powder. You will then select some extras—the garnish, so to speak, of your wash. If you live in a hard-water area (see chapter 7), you might reach for a water softener, which will allow you to use less detergent and will make your clothes less harsh on the skin. You might put in a fabric conditioner, which is so important for . . . well, sort of fluffing up the fibers on the clothes. If there's any danger at all of color running in the wash, you will guard against it by putting a "color catcher" in with the clothes.

Rather than forgetting all about the wash you've put in until reminded of it three days later by your son shouting, "Dad, I haven't got any trousers!" you will make sure you are right beside the machine when the spin cycle ends and the wash is complete. You may even have deliberately chosen to buy a washing machine that, when the wash has ended, beeps continually until you switch it off (as opposed to buying one of these by accident and spending hours futilely scanning the in-structions for a way of disabling the beep, which is what I did). You will favor this facility because you will know that some clothes develop stubborn creases if left dry-ing in the machine.

Next, instead of just stuffing everything into the dryer

before the commercials are over, you will deposit only the clothes that are *supposed* to be put into the dryer. (See the section Do I Need to Bother About the Labels on the Clothes?). Others you will hang on the line in the garden, or drape over a clotheshorse, or lie flat according to the type of fiber. But you will never dry clothes over a radiator because that makes them go hard.

My wife always dries the clothes on the radiators, and it was after I'd told her, for the third or fourth time, "You're not supposed to do that, you know," that she graciously invited me to take over the weekly wash myself. She is not one of the fastidious kinds of clothes washers described previously. She does the *washing* rather than the *laundry*, in other words. She keeps only one washing powder (biological, "because it's stronger") and, apart from a bit of dabbling with fabric conditioner, she takes the minimalist approach that I now commend to my readers.

PUTTING A LOAD IN

In laundry—and only in laundry—apartheid is a good thing. Your whites should be washed separately from your coloreds. Most of your whites will be cotton whites—shirts, sheets, and pillowcases—and you can get away with murder here. There is no danger of color run (white is not a color, you see), and they can be washed on any setting from the lowest temperature to the highest, which is 90 degrees Celsius* and called a boil wash in the UK even though it is not boiling.

"What about things that are both white and colored?" I hear. Put them in with coloreds. Then, if they do run, they're less likely to ruin the whole wash than if you'd put them in with whites—and remember that your aim is not to ruin the whole wash. Anything short of ruining the whole wash can be counted as a success. Higher temperature settings give a better wash, but they wear out—and may fade—the clothes faster. On the face of it, hot washes are less environmentally friendly than cool ones (but see the section Lunch with the Woman Who's Washed More Than 120,000 Socks), and they bring a greater danger of shrinkage and color run.

I asked my wife about her approach to temperature settings:

"Sixty degrees for whites, forty degrees for coloreds. Woolens on the woolen cycle."

I had expected a longer and more nuanced answer.

"Hold on," I said, "what about . . . ?"

She held up her hand.

"I'm not prepared to defend it or talk about it any more. It's what I've always done, what I always will do, and it works fine."

---

* 194 degrees Fahrenheit.

DO I NEED TO BOTHER ABOUT
THE LABELS ON THE CLOTHES?

The awkward fact is that the label is always there, and will still be there reproaching you after the trousers have shrunk to plus fours or after the whole of your wash has been dyed red by a rogue T-shirt bought for a pound on holiday. They're called "care instructions," and the implication is that if you don't look at them, you don't care. Some labels are more comprehensive than others. There's practically an essay written inside clothes bought from those goody-goodies at Marks and Spencer. Other times, you just get the basic symbols. Decode these hieroglyphics by looking on the Internet at, for example, www.carelabelling.co.uk (or www.laundrycaresymbols.com). The essentials are that the number given inside the little drawing of a washtub is the maximum temperature at which the garment should be washed. An image showing hands inside the tub means "hand wash only." The triangle refers to bleaching instructions: you can ignore this provided you also ignore bleach (which I urge you to do). A circle means you can dry-clean the item. A circle in a square means you can tumble dry it. A cross through any of these means you can't do it.

The bottom line—I repeat—is that if you wash too hot, you risk color run, shrinkage, or both. Some very colorful garments bear the words *Wash strong colors separately*, which could mean that you can wash a collection of colorful items all at once or that you should wash each individual one on its own. It's a calculated ambiguity meant to stop you from suing the manufacturer. Fear of litigation means that care labels, like directions on medicines, tend toward the excessively cautious, but if your colors do run, and you attempt to rectify the problem with bleach or some proprietary color-run remover, then you're into GCSE*-level chemistry and beyond the reach of this book. I mean . . . good luck to you, pal.

LUNCH WITH THE WOMAN WHO'S WASHED MORE THAN 120,000 SOCKS

I first met Anne at a dinner party in Highgate. She is an attractive, immediately and obviously competent woman in early middle age. I told her I was interested in washing, and she said, "Really? That's highly unusual for a man. It's highly unusual for anyone. . . . I'm *very* interested in washing."

Which is just as well since Anne has "washed over 120,000 socks so far, and every time one of my four children has a birthday, I update them on the figure. I feel that I was a washerwoman in a previous life. I've washed clothes on stones on the banks of the Ganges—"

"Not literally?" I put in.

---

* The equivalent in the UK of the SAT in the United States.

"Yes, literally. It was in my gap year. I've washed clothes in many rivers, actually. Laundry has always been an interest of mine, and I think a lot of *women* need help with it, never mind men. Of course, the media take no interest at all. I once put up the idea of a radio series on washing, and there was just this long silence, but I mean . . . how do I know how to wash an acrylic-nylon mixture? How would I know how to wash something that's, for example, twenty percent nylon, twenty percent gingham, twenty percent mohair, twenty percent elastane, and twenty percent elastodiene?'

"Well," I said, "you could look at the label."

"Ha!" she said, and it began to occur to me that I might be in the presence of someone who knew more about laundry than the people who write the labels.

I invited myself to lunch with Anne in order to discuss laundry. She's married to a solicitor, and he must be a good one because they live in what seems like a grand Georgian farmhouse set down in the middle of Hampstead.

"I am a housewife," she said, handing me a glass of juice, "because I'm not in paid employment and there's no other term for what I do. But I have four children, and it's a full-time job running this household."

Anne has a daily woman to help out, of course, but she reserves the washing of the clothes for herself.

"It began when I was a teenager. I wanted to manage my own clothes. It's so hard to find an item of clothing that really works for you, and when you do get one, you want to look after it."

Before serving lunch, she showed me her laboratory-like laundry room, where the washing machine was quietly, almost thoughtfully, clicking its way through a cycle. On shelves above it, various detergents and stain removers were not so much stored as filed. I was about to blurt out, "We only use one detergent in our house," but that seemed a slander on my wife, so I modified my remark: "We . . . don't have as many as you."

Anne uses mainly nonbiological detergents, believing that biological is bad for the skin. She also believes that detergents in liquid form are less harsh. She showed me some of her specialist stain removers: she has one for grass stains, one for coffee and tea, and one for blood. I said that it seemed a bit ghoulish to have gone out and bought a stain remover especially for blood.

"With women, blood is quite a big issue," she said.

"Oh," I said, going red, "of course."

She uses fabric conditioner (what you know as fabric softener) because it makes the clothes easier to iron and more comfortable to wear. But not for towels: "They become less absorbent."

No fabric conditioner on towels? That was a bit of a shock. I told Anne that, as a boy, I'd often seen TV commercials for a fabric conditioner that contrasted a drawerful of towels washed without conditioner—they looked dead—with a drawerful washed with conditioner, and these barely fit into the drawer; they had to be lovingly suppressed by the manicured hand of the proud housewife.

"Well," said Anne, "you have to make your own decisions. A lot of labels, for example, will lazily say 'hand wash only' when it's perfectly all right to put the garment in the machine."

"It's more environmentally friendly to wash at a cooler setting, isn't it?" I said, trying to prove that I knew *something*.

"Yes," she said, "but not if you have to wash the clothes more often. And you can use less detergent in a hotter wash."

"Of course, one has to empty all the pockets out before doing a wash," I said.

"Absolutely," said Anne. "Especially with black jeans. If you leave a white tissue in a pair of black jeans, you're picking the white specks off for weeks."

"Yes," I said, "we've all been there." (Although in fact I hadn't.)

"About drying . . ." I said.

"Tumble-dryers are fine," said Anne, "but use with caution. Just look at all the fibers that collect in the filters—that's your clothes that are falling apart in there."

Anne prefers to dry her clothes on her extensive collection of clotheshorses (she's got a whole stable of them) or on the wooden racks hanging from the ceiling of her laundry room, which are similar to the ones we had in our kitchen when I was a child. The difference is that Anne knows what they are called: Dutch airers.

"You dry woolens by laying them flat, don't you?" I cautiously suggested.

"Well, you can put them over a clotheshorse," said Anne, "but you mustn't let the sleeves dangle, because they *will* stretch."

I suggested that you could dry woolens by stretching a towel across the top of a clothes horse and laying the garment on top, and she was polite enough to nod and say, "Absolutely."

As we finished our lunch, Anne suggested two things that men might do to ease the burden of laundry on women. One, they might actually do the laundry, and, two, they might buy shirts enabling the old-fashioned practice of changing collars and cuffs every day rather than the whole shirt.

"People generally change their clothes far too often, don't they?" I said.

"Of course," she replied, "hence the 120,000 socks."

HOW CAN I KEEP MY SOCKS TOGETHER?

Anne has a special basket for odd socks, and there were three hundred socks in it when I visited it. My own collection runs to about twenty-five, but the number climbs after almost every wash. They are the socks of everyone in the family, but they are my problem, because in taking on the family wash I have taken on the unmatched socks.

As I load socks into the washing machine, I know it's "good-bye" rather than "au revoir" to anything up to a quarter of the damn things. The remaining halves are then tied in a bundle (a long-widowed red football sock doing duty as twine) and kept on the shelf above the washing machine. Some have been in the bundle for a couple of years, and any hope of finding the partner has all but disappeared; the trail has gone completely cold. But of course I know that as soon as I throw out any one of my single socks, the other one in the pair will turn up.

Miles, a friend of mine, said that he went looking all around the house every few weeks trying to match up socks.

"It's quite good fun, actually. It's like that game of solitaire where you have to find pairs."

"I suppose that when you find one, you're overjoyed."

He nodded: "It's like the prodigal son."

"Where do they go, do you find?"

"Oh, they get paired up with other socks; get caught in sleeves and trouser legs; drop down behind the washing machine, behind the dryer. They drop off the clothesline and go into the bushes. They get inside pillowcases . . . and sometimes," he added, with a look of wonderment, "one sock will go completely inside another."

I told Miles that I thought the pairing of socks satisfied a particularly male desire for logic and order.

"Could be," he said. "My wife never bothers about it at all."

(Later on, his wife told me that "pairing socks is the only work Miles ever does about the house.")

My own wife has a very lax definition of a "pair" of socks. She'll think nothing of putting a light blue ribbed sock with a slightly shorter *gray* ribbed sock. The children have "fun" days-of-the-week socks, which are black except for the days of the week written in different colors, and my wife will put Tuesday (beige) with Sunday (purple) in a completely irresponsible way. "It's near enough," she'll say.

While telephoning Anne to thank her for our laundry lunch, I brought up the single-sock question.

"Don't worry about it. It's completely normal."

"But I do worry about it. Should I try tucking them into pairs before the wash?"

"They'll come apart in the spin cycle," she said.

"It's incredible that no one's thought of a solution to this problem."

"Look," she said, "buy cheap socks. But you could hold your best ones together by joining them with a couple of stitches."

"No," I said after a pause for thought, "I'm not going to do that."

"Then you want a laundry bag."

"A what?"

She explained that these were net bags.*

You put into them the items of laundry you particularly wanted to see again, and then put the bags into the washing machine.

The next day, I went to John Lewis on Oxford Street and asked a young male assistant, "Have you got any laundry bags?"

"Do you want them for . . . protecting . . . women's . . . underwear?" he asked, his confidence faltering with each successive word.

"No," I said. "I want them for keeping socks together."

"Oh, okay," he said.

Was he just humoring me, or was this a normal requirement?

I asked him.

"Quite normal," he said, tapping something into a computer. "But I see that we're right out of laundry bags just now."

"Do you sell a lot of laundry bags?"

"Hundreds."

"Have you ever sold one to a man?"

"To be honest, not very often."

He was a diplomatic fellow.

---

* Rather more seductively named "lingerie bags" in America.

3

Ironing

WHY DO THE IRONING?

In her book, *A Woman's Work Is Never Done*, Caroline Davidson acknowledged that "Increasing numbers of men, especially in the middle classes, have started to cook, shop and wash-up, many with evident enjoyment. But the ancient taboos against men doing cleaning and hand laundry remain almost as strong as ever."

To most men, ironing is beyond the pale. Both my brother-in-law and my friend Stewart absolutely won't do any ironing at all. I ask why, and there's just a curt shake of the head—they don't even want to *talk* about why they won't do any ironing. What these men have in common is that they work at home and so don't need to look smart every day. They don't lead with their shirtfronts. They do *wear* shirts, and usually good-quality cotton ones at that (the hardest to keep flat), but they wear them with the creases concealed beneath turtleneck sweaters. Stewart and my brother-in-law evidently think that ironing is effeminate, whereas I think that wearing turtleneck sweaters is effeminate. Turtleneck sweaters are portable central heating: modern, sensible, soft, and not endorsed by any male role model that I know of. I mean, does James Bond wear a turtleneck sweater?

I admit that, by the same token, there are hardly any prominent men associated with ironing. There's a lot of ironing in the French Foreign Legion apparently, but they're a funny lot. John Osborne was praised for putting an ironing board (next best thing to a kitchen sink) on the stage in *Look Back in Anger*, but it was a woman who did the ironing in the play: the put-upon and much-shouted-at Alison. The only candidate I could come up with was Robert Plant, lead singer of Led Zeppelin, who wanted an ironing board in his dressing room before the group's recent reunion gig in London. He said that ironing "got him in the mood."

All of the members of Led Zeppelin looked well pressed on stage. They evidently knew that the more crumpled a man's face, the smoother his clothes must be. At the age of forty-five, I've squared up to the truth that one common denominator applies whenever I'm complimented on my appearance: my shirt has been properly ironed.

You could get your wife or partner to do all of your ironing. Well, I mean you could try asking, but of the twenty women interviewed by Dr. Gatrell in *Hard Labour*, only two did not object to ironing their partners' shirts. Dr. Gatrell speculates that the ironing of men's shirts is symbolic of "wifework" in that it "promotes her husband's business lifestyle at the expense of her own." In any case, your wife does not have the same interest in your looking good in public as you do yourself—in fact, it might be considered directly contrary to her interests. You could take your most flattering shirts to the laundry, and that's what I used to do, at a cost of nine pounds for three, to be washed and ironed. I would usually pay with a credit card, and it was a notice posted to the counter that drove me away from the place: "A charge of 50p <u>will</u> be made for every credit card transaction under ten pounds." It was the underlining of the word *will* that did it.

Once you are ironing your own clothes, you might as well take on the whole family's. Make the offer to your wife. I should think she might just take you up on it, unless you're hooked up to one of those fastidious ironers—one of those women who irons, say, linen by a process so refined that the iron at no point makes contact with the material. Yes, it's a lot of work: a family of four generates between three and six hours of ironing a week. But in taking on the ironing you will in a single stroke have punctured one of your wife's biggest grievances, which will be as much to your benefit as hers. No longer will she be able to lever the old "Do you know how long I've spent doing the ironing this week?" into your disputes. That particular weapon is now in your hands.

And it's not that difficult. Even clothes ironed by an undomesticated man really do look ironed, at least from a distance of about ten feet, and there is something satisfying in making clothes stackable. If, like me, you tend to drink too much wine of an evening, then ironing also puts a check on that. I suppose there are some very decadent men who iron while sitting down—or even in bed—with bottle, glass, and ashtray wobbling on the ironing board. But I iron standing up (which has to be good for me) and with my wineglass some distance away on the mantelpiece. *I'll have another sip*, I'll tell myself, *after I've done these next three shirts*. Anyone entering the room would think I'd completely forgotten about the glass. And I find that once I've started ironing, I don't want to stop, and when I return to my white wine after a long session at the board, I often find it's gone completely warm.

I'll get to the bottom of the ironing basket and I won't want to stop. I'll see little runtish, long-neglected scraps of things: stray napkins, anomalous doily-type things of my wife's, all mangled and creased, and I'll think, *Right, soon have these sorted out*, and I'll completely flatten them and put them on the dining room table, where I stack all of my ironing for my wife to put away. (Because, although I iron everything, I don't know where it all goes.) And then, rather than pack up the ironing board, I might start wandering around the house looking for other things to iron, and I have once or twice reached the world-turned-upside-down situation with my wife in which she has felt the need to ask, "Will you please *stop* ironing?"

Another good thing about ironing is that you can do other things at the same time. A radio producer once told me that radio was a superior medium to television because "the radio audience is very active." When I asked what exactly he meant by this, he became shifty, but I eventually forced him to admit that he meant they were doing other things while listening—that they were actually not really listening at all. My dad irons while watching the racing on television on weekday afternoons. The only other man I know who irons as much as I do does it on Saturday afternoon while listening to football on the radio. I myself always watch a DVD while ironing, and I note an interesting discrepancy between the subject matter of the sorts of films I like and the domesticated mildness of the act of ironing: some criminal will be getting his head shot off while I'm carefully aligning the creases on my youngest son's school trousers; as the putrefying zombie makes its climactic appearance, I'll be squinting at the care label on one of my wife's blouses. (You can't watch subtitled DVDs while ironing, incidentally, or at least not while ironing properly.)

I iron in one or two weekly sessions, but my wife will occasionally walk into my study while I'm working and ask me to do a couple of quick one-off jobs—a shirt for one of the boys who might be going somewhere particularly smart, for instance. She knows she's pushing her luck, and that I will extract my price. "I'll do it sometime in the next hour," I'll say. "Thanks, Andrew," she'll reply, and as she turns to go, I'll call after her, "Now, you'll set the iron up, won't you? And you'll have the trousers all ready on the ironing board?"

HOW TO GET THINGS REALLY FLAT

When I first did the ironing, my wife said she would help me put the ironed clothes away. On the second or third occasion, she said, "I'm very grateful to you for doing this, you know."

"But what do you think of the actual ironing?"

"It's very bad. It's very . . . cavalier."

Not that she was bothered. Most of the things I iron are the boys' school shirts and trousers, and these are worn for one day before being carefully rolled into a ball and left in an inch of dirty water on the bathroom floor. The next biggest category was my own shirts—or at least the ones my wife had entrusted me with. Every week she'd take three of the better ones to the local laundry for pressing, and she'd instruct me to wear one of these whenever I went to an important social occasion (i.e., one involving her friends).

It was depressing to compare the dozen or so of my

shirts that I'd ironed with these three done professionally, and I became haunted by a label on one of my better shirts that made a mockery of my efforts by airily instructing, "Launder commercially."

But then, about a month into my ironing career, a stylish, rather astringent woman came around to our house—I'll call her Helena. We were sipping champagne before Sunday lunch, and I asked, "Do you know anything about ironing?"

"Well . . . yes," she said—and very warily, because it is just about the most fraught question you can ask a modern woman.

Emboldened by my aperitif, I said, "I'd like you to come into the bedroom and look at my shirts. . . . Tell me what you think about the quality of the ironing."

"All right," she said, after a longish pause.

We walked through to the bedroom; I opened the wardrobe door and showed her the disreputable parade. She looked at my shirts in silence for a while, unsmiling.

"First of all," she said, "they're all hung up far too close together. They're all pressing against each other."

'Well, that's easily fixed," I said, but as I spoke the words, I wondered how, since we were at the limit of our bedroom cupboard space.

"You could get rid of a few of them," said Helena, still eyeing the shirts, ". . . quite a lot of them, in fact."

"I think this one's come out quite well," I said, reaching for my favorite white shirt. "It always does."

I took it off the hanger so that she could look more closely.

"It's poly-cotton," she said, glancing at the label.

"It's an old shirt," I said. "Someone gave it to me—I've always liked it."

"Well, it's dead," she said.

"How do you mean?"

"The fabric. It's completely dead."

"Is that because it's polyester-cotton rather than pure cotton? Or is it just because it's old?"

"I should say both."

"Right," I said, a bit taken aback, "but it irons well."

"That's because it's got poly in it. It's a kind of plastic."

"I've seen 'easy-iron' shirts advertised in shops. Is that what they're made of, poly-cotton?"

She nodded.

"But I prefer *cotton* shirts," I said.

"So do I," she said, which was just about the first positive remark she'd made. "Cotton shirts always look better," she continued, ". . . if they're properly ironed."

"I thought the trouble might be that I wasn't ironing both sides of the fabric."

"What?" she said.

"I was reading an old copy of *Good Housekeeping*—from the 1930s in the British Library—and it said you should iron both sides of a cotton garment."

Helena just seemed entirely nonplussed by that.

"Listen," she said. "Have you got one of those clear plastic bottles with a sprayer on top?"

"The kind of thing you use to spray houseplants, you mean?"

"Yes."

"No, I haven't."

"Get one. Spray the shirt for a few seconds. Don't soak it. Then roll it up like a scroll and leave it for a few minutes so that the moisture goes to all parts of the shirt. Do that with all the shirts before you start ironing, and use the sprayer on everything else that's hard to iron."

"Right," I said. "I'll give it a try."

"Do you know how to iron a shirt?" she went on, and the question was clearly rhetorical, because she immediately took down one of my shirts and answered it herself: "You should be stretching the fabric all the time as you go. The collars and cuffs are double thickness, so you can do them first because they won't come unironed by the manipulation of the rest of the shirt. People say you should do the collar from the center to one edge, and then the center again to the other edge, but nobody bothers about that. Just unfold it and do it straight across from one side to the other. You should do both sides of the collar, and you should do the front of it first."

"Why?" I interrupted.

"Because then the corners will tend to curl in the right direction . . . look, don't worry about it. After the collar, do the cuffs, both sides, then the sleeves, working out from the shoulders. Do the yoke of the shirt next, on the edge of the board. The yoke is that bit between the collar and the horizontal seam running three inches below it.

Then do the back of the shirt last, because that's the bit most likely to come unironed. You can then fold it, and iron in the creases, but I wouldn't bother trying if I were you. Some men like to put on a folded shirt. But it must be folded properly."

I told Helena that I'd noticed that the proper way to fold a shirt—pulling the sleeves behind as if it's being arrested by a policeman—is also the most difficult.

"It takes a bit of practice. It's just as good to hang it straight up . . . on a wooden hanger. Half of yours are bent metal ones."

(There was no denying *that*.)

"Aren't wooden hangers very expensive?"

"You can get four for a pound if you know where to look."

And there it all is. And it works.

Or at least . . . my shirts have begun to look reasonably good from close up. But there were further matters I wanted to resolve in my pursuit of total flatness.

CORRECT ATTITUDE TOWARD EASY-IRON SHIRTS

Helena seemed to look down on them, but the thing about easy-iron shirts is that they are very easy to iron, and while Helena is an extremely aesthetic person, she is also a woman, and I wanted a man's view.

The most particularly British and gentlemanly of

the many such menswear shops in Jermyn Street, London SW1, is Turnbull and Asser, and it was there that I went for a second opinion. If James Bond actually existed, he would be a regular at Turnbull and Asser, or so the shop—which has supplied ties and shirts to the various on-screen impersonators of Bond—would like us all to think. Here, they will make you a shirt at the drop of a hat, if you can afford it. The handkerchiefs and bow ties are displayed in glass cases like prized exhibits and subdivided according to the season or time of day to be worn, type and weight of silk, and so on. The prospective purchaser is invited to browse through sumptuous volumes detailing, for instance, the evolution of the Duke of Windsor's taste in collars and ties, or the outfits of Cary Grant, or the general refinements of a particularly English way of upper-class dressing.

The assistants at Turnbull and Asser look as though they have stepped from the pages of these books and are sometimes to be seen smoking aesthetically outside the shop.

I walked up to a dapper man lounging against a counter. His hair was perfect; his cuff lengths appeared to have been gauged by a micrometer. I asked: "Do you ever sell easy-iron shirts?'

"Not really, sir."

"I mean polyester-cotton ones."

"I know what you mean, sir."

"Why are they easier to iron?"

"Well," he said, "there's a plastic in the shirt: polyester, I mean . . . it's an American thing."

(Did I detect a slight shudder as he said that?)

"What's wrong with them?"

A flicker of exasperation crossed his face.

"They don't look as good," he said. "They're not as comfortable on the skin, and they don't breathe as well as cotton, so you soon start to sweat in them."

"But they're easier to iron."

"Yes, but anybody with any money doesn't worry about that, do they, sir?"

"Because they pay someone to do the ironing for them."

"Exactly."

I should have known what to expect in Turnbull and Asser. I once asked another assistant there what he thought of made-up bow ties; in reply he turned aside and mimed spitting on the ground.

DO I NEED TO BOTHER ABOUT THE CONTROLS ON THE IRON?

The golden rule here is to try to read the ironing instructions *before* ironing the garment rather than afterward.

Ironing instructions on clothes labels are very simple, unlike the washing instructions discussed earlier. The iron symbol employed is simply a drawing of a small iron, and the manufacturers of clothes obviously got together at some stage with the manufacturers of irons to agree on a system that even most men will be able to understand. If you're not supposed to iron the thing at all, then the little iron is crossed out. Two dots inside the little iron mean you set the thermostat of the iron to two dots. If you iron things too cool, you won't harm them, but they just won't go flat. If you iron certain man-made fibers too hot, they might start smoking and melting, in which case my advice would be to *stop* ironing them.

A danger of ironing woolen garments at too high a temperature is that they become shiny, and a shiny patch on a good woolen suit indicates a man in decline. You might consider ironing woolens through a thin piece of muslin, slightly dampened. My father used to do this.

Manufacturers play safe by instructing you to use a cooler setting than strictly necessary. Or so I like to think because it is unquestionably more fun—and quicker—to iron hot. I have always ironed my sons' school trousers (polyester viscose) on a three-dot setting rather than the two that are recommended—no harm done that I can see.

When I first started to pay attention to the washing and ironing instructions, it occurred to me that the clothes had lasted perfectly well up to that point. Perhaps this was because my wife had been paying attention to the labels? But when I ran this idea past her, she said that she only "sort of" looked at them. Some of the labels had in any case faded away almost to nothing because it is possible, oddly enough, for the care instructions to be washed off over time. I once hauled a pair of sports trousers belonging to one of the boys from the ready-for-ironing basket, and the label read: "Keep away from . . ." with the final word completely obliterated. I decided to put them straight back into the basket, just in case the last word had been "irons" (or perhaps there had originally been three words: "men with irons"). Once you're doing the bulk of the household ironing, no one's going to blame you for not ironing any particular item, whereas you could lose all the credit you've earned in taking on the job by putting a hole—even quite a small one—in your wife's best cashmere sweater. The golden rules, incidentally, regarding women's cashmere sweaters, are as follows: do not attempt to wash them or iron them. Do not touch them; do not even go near them, lest you be accused of damaging them in some way.

As you acquire some knowledge of laundering, you might become equally protective of your own favorite items, and it seems to be that the principles of the free market operate effectively in this area. Whereas in my early boyhood the acquisition of a new pair of flared green cords would be one of the events of the year, clothes are relatively cheap these days. People can afford to shrug off their loss. But any garment worth protecting from the rigors of the laundry will be so protected. Somebody will be looking out for it, and counseling caution, or furtively whisking it away for the more considered attentions of the dry-cleaner.

WHAT IS STARCH, AND DOES IT REALLY MATTER?

I knew that some men wore starched shirts—just as some people slept on starched sheets and pillowcases—but this seemed severe to me. I had never seen anybody using starch in ironing, and wasn't it for dandies only? I would begin by finding out what it was.

Under the kitchen sink, in among my wife's thicket of cleaning lotions, I discovered "spray starch." It contained, according to the bottle, "natural starch," which didn't get me any further. I asked my wife, "What is starch?"

"I don't know. It might be flour and water."

I asked her what she used it for, and she said she put it on the double damask napkins (whatever they are).

All I knew about starch was that it appeared in food and glue, and I didn't want to put anything like food or glue onto my shirts. Later that day, in the London Library, I consulted that Victorian domestic bible, *Mrs Beeton's Book of Household Management*, which was first published in 1869. The entry on "How to Make Starch" began: "Put the starch into a tolerably large basin. . . ."

And so the mystery was perpetuated. Starch, it seemed, just *is*. I next tried the monumental and definitive *Home Comforts: The Art and Science of Keeping House*, by the American lawyer, philosopher, and housework maven Cheryl Mendelson, and looked up "Starches and Sizings." "Starches are plant starches," Ms. Mendelson began, somewhat self-reflexively, "but formerly wheat or potato starch and other substances were commonly used." I then looked up the Wikipedia entry. "Starch," I read, "is a mixture of amylase and amylopectin, usually in 20:80 or 30:70 ratios. These are both complex carbohydrate polymers of glucose, making starch a glucose polymer as well, as seen in the chemical formula for starch, regardless of the ratio of amylase/amylopectin."

Mmm . . .

Returning to our own spray can, I saw that it was running low, so I went to the hardware shop to buy some more.

"We do have old-fashioned starch, you know," said the shopkeeper. "The kind you make up in hot water."

This was the kind Mrs. Beeton was talking about. But I said that the spray starch would do for me, and before first incorporating starch into my ironing routine, I called the phone number printed on the can of spray starch "for friendly and expert advice." I got through to an answering machine and was invited to leave a message. I did so, explaining that, as a first-time starch user, I was looking for general advice on when and where to use the stuff.

A week later, not having received a reply to my message (indeed, I was still waiting for a reply at the time of this book's printing), I began my first experiment with it. I held the can at 45 degrees as instructed on the label, and sprayed the starch onto a shirt which I had already moistened according to the instructions of Helena as set out above . . . and I found that the whole experience of ironing the shirt was now different. The iron seemed to roll over a veneer, and there was an indestructible look to the flatness of the shirt when I'd finished. In fact, the shirt looked professionally ironed from as close up as about five feet.

But starch, especially spray starch, is not cheap. I keep it for my best shirts, just as my wife keeps it for her best napkins.

WHAT IS A STEAM GENERATOR IRON,* AND DO I NEED ONE?

Steam is the key to successful ironing. I once asked my wife why, and she said, "It's something to do with the way it affects the fabric."

"Yes," I said, "well, it would be, wouldn't it?"

"Look it up on the Internet," she said.

I found out that steam works because it loosens the bonds between the fibers (or something like that).

---

* These seem to be called "pressure irons" or "steam pressure irons" in America. From the tenor of American Internet discourse about them—many people frankly asking, "What is a steam pressure iron?"—I see that they are only slowly gaining hold there, as is the case in Britain.

Anyway, steam generator irons refine the use of steam. They were pioneered by the well-dressed Italians in the late 1970s, but they began to catch on in Britain only fifteen or so years ago. They are irons attached to a water tank that is about the size of a big casserole pot. This generates "dry steam," which is hotter than the steam made in an ordinary steam iron.

This dry steam, and the fact that the water tanks last for an hour before needing to be refilled, means that ironing is quicker. Steam generators also enable "vertical ironing," whereby the garment is hung up, or held up by hand, and the creases fall out of it only when the steaming iron is brought *near*.

I was asking about steam irons in John Lewis on Oxford Street, and the assistant led me over to where she had a basketful of creased shirts and an ironing board all set up. It might seem strange, incidentally, to come upon this little domestic tableau in the bustle of an Oxford Street store, but the female assistants in John Lewis (and in fact some of the male ones) are so reassuringly maternal that you can easily imagine them getting on with a spot of ironing in between serving customers. The assistant—Sandra by name—held a cotton shirt near the iron and the creases fell out of it more or less immediately.

"So, with this iron, you don't need to iron anything?" I said, amazed.

"It's even better if you do," she said, and she ran the

iron quickly over another shirt, making it flat in very short order.

Sandra explained that the volume and pressure of the steam meant that no physical pressure on the iron was necessary. "You don't even need to spray on water?" I said.

"Certainly not."

The iron she was using cost about a hundred and eighty pounds in the UK, whereas an ordinary steam iron costs about half that. "But you'll iron everything at least twice as quickly," said Sandra, "and you know when you iron your shirts, and they look really good in the wardrobe, but when you go back the next day a lot of the creases somehow mysteriously come back?"

"Yes?" I said excitedly, because she had identified my number-one outstanding ironing problem: the tendency of my shirts to become unironed during the night.

"Well, with this, you just get the iron out for a minute, wave it in front of them, and they're back to how they were."

My only doubt was over that matter of "whipping the iron out" for a minute. A steam generator iron is a bit like an iron on a dialysis machine. It might get through the ironing twice as fast, but I think it would take about twice as long to set up as an ordinary iron and would be that much more inconvenient to carry toward the ironing board, with the result that I might be about *half* as likely to use it. At the moment I don't know of any woman who owns a steam generator iron, let alone a man. But they are the future of ironing.

WHAT IS THE WORST THING THAT CAN HAPPEN DURING IRONING?

You could ruin a garment by ironing on too high a temperature. You could, if you weren't paying attention, ruin a number of them. A bit of melted man-made fiber might accumulate on the sole plate of your iron, and you might transfer this to your best white shirt. Irons can be cleaned with proprietary iron cleaners, and I once cleaned mine perfectly satisfactorily with warm water and dishwashing liquid.

As a test at the start of a session, always iron something you don't care about—something that is not yours, in other words.

Let me see now . . .

You could fatally electrocute yourself with a steam iron that had become faulty, or you could injure someone else—perhaps another man, curious about this piece of exotic equipment. For instance, most steam irons have a facility enabling a sort of bonus jet of steam to be fired out of the sole plate onto particularly stubborn creases. It's sometimes called a steam burst. You could be holding the iron vertically and demonstrating this to someone. "Look closer," you say, "and you'll see where the steam comes out. . . ."

But by far the most likely thing is that you will start a fire as a result of forgetting to upend the iron when called away unexpectedly from the ironing board. You are ironing when the phone rings . . . or someone knocks at the door . . . or you feel the urge to make a cup of tea. These are the danger points for any man at the ironing board, to whom any interruption is likely to be more diverting than the task of ironing. Before dashing away, stand the iron up.

4

Washing Up*

* Or, "Doing the Dishes"

WHY WASH UP?

I assume that any man who does not do any cooking must be bringing home such mountains of cash that his wife or partner is never emboldened, when he steps out of line, to announce: "If you don't behave, I won't feed you." (Because I've often thought of saying that to my children.) In any case, washing up—a.k.a. doing the dishes, or loading the dishwasher—is the least that a man can do. It's like paying the bill; it draws a line under the meal.

But there is another, better reason for doing the washing up, which is that it gets you out of irksome social situations. At any gathering of what the advertisers call "family and friends," home truths will begin to be bandied after a certain amount of wine has gone down, or things will become otherwise strained. I never like being asked how I am, and toward the end of a meal, people will begin fiddling with their empty wineglasses while enquiring, "But Andrew, how *are* you?" as though all my earlier responses had conveyed something less than the full truth on this point. Instead of saying, "I am perfectly all right, thank you, now please shut up," I convey the same message in more diplomatic terms: "I'm just off to do the washing up," I say.

I might notice some of the women at the table actually nodding in approval at this. Others are wise to my gambit and are ambivalent about it. *How boorish,* I can see them thinking as I rise from the table. *He hasn't the good grace to sit and make a little small talk with his friends and family . . . and yet on the other hand, he is going to do the washing up . . . I wish my other half would do that.* They're torn about it, you can tell. Later on, they might come through to the kitchen to check whether I *am* actually doing the washing up, and I *will* be doing it, not least of all because it's enjoyable.

I often do the washing up with my dad, who's just as antisocial as I am. I wash and he dries, and it is understood between us that, as dryer, he will charitably wipe off any stains or indeed lumps of food that might be left on the crockery or cutlery after I've hauled it from the washing bowl. Sometimes, if for example a knife is positively clarted—as we Yorkshiremen say—

with chocolate pudding, he might frown at it and pass it back, saying in a confidential tone, "I'd give that another going-over if I were you."

I always think it's very magnanimous of him to let me wash up, because that's the senior role. A man washing up secretly imagines himself to be the head surgeon in an operating theater. He is entitled to bark out peremptory orders: "Right! I'm ready for the pudding things now!" And ten minutes into the job, he will probably find that he has accumulated a whole team of helpers, in the shape of all the antisocial men who've slunk away from the dinner table.

The male washer-up takes pride in the increasing filthiness of his washing-up water, just as his colleague at the draining board savors the increasing sogginess of his tea towel. I have seen my dad wringing out his tea towel before making a start on the wineglasses, while I might indicate to him the washing bowl and its contents resembling minestrone soup. "Just look at all the stuff we're getting off these pots, Dad," I'll say, and he'll nod in satisfaction.

I once tried to explain to my wife the pleasure I felt in washing up: "It's a lot to do with simply having your hands in warm water—something to do with an unconscious memory of amniotic fluid. The other thing is just the enjoyment of performing a simple physical task."

"Yes," she said, "only it's not quite as simple as you imagine."

EXEMPLARY WASHING UP

Sometimes, a couple of hours after I've finished the washing up and when, having wrested the conversation around to subjects of my own choosing, I'm well into my second bottle of wine, I will pause and note the gentle sound of running water and soft singing coming from the direction of the kitchen.

This is my wife, doing the washing up all over again.

Whereas she is relaxed about the laundry, and positively happy to let me do the ironing and the vacuuming, she has strong feelings about washing up. While some women hanker after a separate laundry room, my wife would like to have a separate washing-up room—an Edwardian scullery—where she could wash up alone, and to the highest standards. I cannot match those standards. Or rather, I can't be bothered to. If I were to examine every glass for grease marks, then washing up would become a trial. Instead, I will examine *some* of the glasses for grease marks—especially the ones that I think won't have any. I know the theory of good washing up but employ it only patchily, so I am much happier washing up when my wife is not watching. I am tormented by the discrepancy between my own performance and the one I know she hankers after seeing. I will now try to convey my wife's dream, or idealized vision of male washing up.

It begins at the dining table, where the vision of her husband pouring himself another glass of white wine while making a willfully provocative statement begins to fade away. The scene goes wobbly . . .

. . . and dissolves to the unexpected image of Andrew solicitously passing around the coffee and chocolates. A few moments later, having explained in full exactly how he is, and having given everybody else the fullest possible opportunity to explain how they are, he graciously excuses himself to everybody in turn and walks through to the kitchen in company with his father.

In the kitchen, Andrew commands two sinks or, failing that, two plastic washing-up basins—one for washing, the other for rinsing—and a draining board. He fills both with water as hot as his hands can stand, but not boiling because (a) his hands can't stand that, and (b) he knows that boiling water cracks glasses. Andrew directs a small squirt of dishwashing liquid into one of the basins—no more than a teaspoon is required—ensuring that the lather is not so thick that he can't see through it. Andrew will start with the glasses: they need the cleanest water.

Andrew's father is readying himself with what he always refers to as a "glass cloth," knowing the expression "tea towel" has long signified suburban naffness. It is made of soft, supple linen or cotton. It is clean, and it is not decorated with an amusingly convoluted account of the rules of cricket, but is pure white. And yet, even though it is a "glass" cloth, Andrew's aim is as follows: he will wash the glasses. He uses a small sink mop to rinse them (checking that the dishwashing liquid has left no grease marks) and then leaves them on the draining board to dry by evaporation alone. This is the way to ensure that they sparkle.

While the glasses are drying, Andrew calls—politely—for the cutlery. Cutlery can tolerate slightly less clean water than the glasses, but of course, Andrew changes the washing and rinsing water regularly in any case. He is careful about the silver, and anything bone-handled. If in doubt, he consults the person who bought this fine cutlery—his wife—who takes the view, not shared by everybody, that bone-handled cutlery can be completely immersed in hot soapy water.

Generally speaking, Andrew's father dries the cutlery as quickly as possible, because he knows that, whether at home in York or at Andrew's place in London, he is in a hard-water area, and that hard water causes marks on metal. Meanwhile, Andrew turns to the crockery. He scrapes any large particles of dirt into the kitchen bin first, and he never scours any good crockery. He knows—because his wife has told him, and he has listened—that bone china has a glaze. This is what makes it beautiful, and it will be rubbed away by scouring.

By the time of the crockery, incidentally, Andrew's father is on his second or third glass cloth. He never hands anything back to Andrew for a second cleaning for the simple reason that nothing comes to him dirty. Pots and pans are next, and Andrew makes a reasoned, executive decision to leave some of them to soak. He knows that it is best to put cold water into a pan besmirched with cooked egg, because hot water will only make the egg set. (This goes for milk and porridge, and all proteins, as Andrew well knows.) A pan with intractable burnt food in the bottom might be filled by Andrew with water and a dash of bicarbonate of soda for soaking overnight. But he knows not to do this with aluminum pans because aluminum reacts with bicarbonate of soda.

Some of the pots and pans—the roasting tin in particular—contain fat. Andrew never pours fat down the sink, having once read that it cools in the sewers, hardens, and forms obstructions that, in 2007 alone, resulted, according to Thames Water, in two thousand homes in Greater London being flooded—and flooded, moreover, with sewage. Instead, he scrapes the fats into some disposable receptacle and puts it in the bin. He doesn't boast about doing this, nor does he feel smug or self-congratulatory about it, because he acknowledges that ideally, if he weren't so busy with house-work, he should have molded the fat into a ball, dotted it with seeds and nuts, and made a bird feeder out of it.

Andrew's father, at the drying station, is in charge of putting away any pots and pans that are cleaned directly, and he is careful to ensure that the undersides of them are absolutely dry, so as to avoid marking the shelves on which they are placed.

Andrew turns to the chopping board. If it's made of wood, he cleans it with hot soapy water but does not leave it to soak because that will blacken and warp it.

At the end of washing up, Andrew leaves the dishcloths to soak in dilute bleach. Both Andrew and his father then dry their hands on a towel—not on the glass cloth, which Andrew's father will have placed in the laundry basket. Andrew's father will then refrain from lighting up a cigarette, and, rather than diving for the corkscrew, Andrew asks whether anyone would like a cup of something like herbal tea.

HOW TO LOAD A DISHWASHER
WITHOUT CAUSING COMMENT

One of the many irksome things about dishwashers is that they will appropriate all of your crockery so that, for about two hours after a dinner party, you have no cups available to use. Since I drink a dozen cups of tea a day, this has often irritated me, and on one occasion I went out and bought a new cup. Then my eldest son told me, "You know you can open the dishwasher in midcycle, and if you close it again, it carries on where it left off.'

"How do you know?" I said, giving him a narrow look.

"Well, I just know."

I tried it. If you open the machine in midcycle, it immediately stops, as though resentful of this party-pooping intervention. It does restart when—having fished out your cup—you close it up again, but only after a sullen pause of a few seconds during which it makes its point: *I may be nominally described as a "convenience," but I am a convenience on my own terms.*

In fact, I should be glad that the dishwasher stops because the alternative would be a faceful of scalding water.

Essentially, a dishwasher takes in cold water, heats it up, filters it through detergent and water softener, then projects it out over the dirty dishes through rotating arms. The dishes are then heated or left to drain, depending on which setting you have selected.

About one in five British households have dishwashers.* My wife and I have one, but we often bypass it and wash up by hand. Until recently I loaded it quickly and, I thought, quite effectively. I would put the lighter things on the top rack, as you are meant to do, with cups and

---

* They are apparently more popular in the United States. Dishwashers are in 70.8 million of the 110.7 occupied housing units in America.

glasses pointing downward. I never put knives point-up in the cutlery basket, having read of a boy who slipped and fell on a knife so placed and was killed. Certainly no fatalities have occurred (so far) as a result of my dishwasher loading, but I came to realize that this was about as much as you could say for it.

I could tell something was amiss from the tendency of other adults in the room to stop what they were doing and to start eyeing me carefully as I went about the job. Conversations would trail off. People might tentatively begin, "If I might just . . ." and then think better of it. Quite often my wife would come over to rearrange the crockery before I started the machine, and one day I asked her if this had anything more to it than ordinary control-freakery. She explained that she was basically separating the things: that china or crockery clashes together under the force of the whirling water.

"And you know why I'm always buying new wooden spoons?" she continued.

"*Are* you?" I said.

"It's because you put them in the dishwasher and they go black."

"Oh," I said. (Certainly I'd noticed the wooden spoons going black, but I thought this was the natural fate of all wooden spoons.)

It seems that you really shouldn't put anything in a dishwasher that was made before dishwashers were invented, which was in 1886.

The drying function of dishwashers can melt plastic, and you must be particularly careful about loading silver and glassware into them. Silver and crystal were made for an age of leisure and elegance. ("They are beautiful," my wife always says, "because they reflect light.") It was intended that they would be cleaned by servants, just as the glass sinks that you will find today in Hampstead and Notting Hill are meant to be cleaned by servants and might indeed be said to exist in order to justify the keeping of them. The dishwasher, with its violently projected very hot water and its strong detergents (both of these enabled by the fact that they will not be coming into contact with human skin), was built for an age of convenience. It could be argued that dishwashers are inimical to beautiful things. They can crack or cloud glass, destroy bone handles, tarnish silver, and take the glaze off bone china, although the more expensive your dishwasher, the more delicate items it will be able to handle. Most dishwashers will have a setting for fine china and glass. There is nothing very sophisticated about this: it is the shortest cycle and can therefore be construed as a tacit admission by the manufacturers of the brutal nature of dishwashers. I used to use this setting for ordinary crockery, just because it gave me a chance of being able to unload the dishwasher during the same kitchen session as the loading. But my wife said it didn't make ordinary crockery clean. I'd never noticed. To my mind, if something had been through a dishwasher cycle, then it was clean by definition.

If I wasn't married, or maybe if I wasn't married to my wife, I wouldn't have a dishwasher. I'd always be able to think of a better way of spending three hundred quid. Dishwashers are quite high maintenance. The water enters them through a water softener—this to make the detergent more effective. In the case of my dishwasher, this water-softening device must be kept topped up with what is referred to as simply "salt." But this is not ordinary salt. It is (guess what?) dishwasher salt, which is very pure, "granular" salt. I need to keep the dishwasher topped up with this, and also with something called rinse-aid, which helps prevent smears forming during drying. My dishwasher features warning lights that flash when salt and rinse-aid are low, and in this sense a dishwasher is like a slot machine, except that when it lights up, it means you're going to spend money rather than receive it.

Incidentally, I know a man who won't have a dishwasher in his house because during his boyhood, his mother would ask him to unload one as a punishment. They have bad associations for me, too. As a teenager I once had a summer job washing dishes in a hotel. Some of the dishes were to be washed by hand; others, in a dishwasher. Throughout the early evenings, herds of pensioners would arrive in coaches operated by the firm Wallace Arnold. The manager would come into the kitchen roaring, "Another Wally in!" and fifty shrimp cocktails would have to be prepared amid much screaming and effing and blinding, while I would have to redouble my efforts at the sink and with the dish-washer, which loosed a great cloud of steam every time I opened it. This would make me reel backward, on the point of fainting, and I would have to remove the plates immediately, even though they were too hot to touch. For years afterward I felt slightly ill whenever I saw a Wallace Arnold coach on the motorway.

5

Vacuuming

WHY VACUUM?

A good friend of mine who is a vicar said that vacuuming is enjoyable for the same reason that cutting the grass, ironing, or dusting is enjoyable: you can see where you've been. (This, I feel, must have figured in a sermon of his at some time.)

When I was a boy, it was my favorite aspect of housework. In the early 1970s, we had an Electrolux vacuum cleaner proudly stored in the broom cupboard in its original box. It looked like a torpedo mounted on little skis, and the hose was speckled like a snake. There was a kind of violence to the machine that I appreciated. Vacuum cleaners were noisier in those days, and while I was ostensibly doing everyone else in the house a favor by vacuuming, I was also making my presence felt.

The moment I switched on the Electrolux, anyone in the house who might happen to have been reading, talking on the phone, watching TV, sleeping, or just pleasantly daydreaming had to immediately stop doing those things. They also had to get out of my way. I prided myself on being able to cover the whole of the house before the motor became dangerously hot, at which point it would prima-donnishly stop working for half an hour, imposing an eerie silence on the house in which everyone twiddled their thumbs.

I would change attachments with the motor still running, and I liked the idea of using the more exotic ones, just as I especially enjoyed those episodes of the British "Supermarionation" classic *Thunderbirds* in which the more obscure rescue craft crawled from the belly of Thunderbird 2: the rarely seen Mole, for example, which rescued people trapped underground, or the even more specialized contraption whose sole function was the stopping of runaway monorail trains. (Actually, I must admit that I never saw that one in action.)

"Going in with the crevice attachment!" I would mutter to myself as I pried open the gap between the sofa cushions and the back of the sofa. I particularly liked the crevice attachment, which is the thinnest of a vacuum cleaner's nozzles. Clipping it onto the cleaner's pipe was like fixing a bayonet, and because of Bernoulli's principle (look it up), it offered the most powerful and concentrated vacuuming. I savored the rapid tingling in the cleaner's pipes as the week's grit, dust, and debris flew miraculously counter to the direction of gravity.

When I deemed the job finished and pressed the Off button, the engine would dwindle gradually like an aircraft engine after landing, and the whole house seemed doubly beautiful in those moments: not only calm, but clean. Standing in the aftermath with one foot proprietarily on the cylinder, I would loop the electric cable like an old sea dog with a hawser and shrug off the fulsome thanks of my father or Mrs. Buffard.

Most of that still applies today, and my appreciation of the value of vacuum cleaners has increased.

I now know that they were invented by Hubert Cecil Booth, who took out his patent in 1901. He had observed a machine used to clean railway carriage seats, which blew rather than sucked and so was *nearly* a brilliant invention. Booth would experiment by putting his mouth to a series of white handkerchiefs placed on the back of a series of dining room chairs and sucking. The handkerchief always came up black.

I also now know that most of the dirt in a house is retained in the carpets. The research department of Hoover once estimated the figure to be as high as 90 percent (but then of course they would say that). And I know that carpets are supposed to last longer if vacuumed at least once a week, and even more frequently in the most used places. I never used to be able to understand why dirt was harmful to carpets. You'd have thought that the dirt already in the carpet was at least stopping any other dirt from getting in, but then Brian, who works in my local vacuum cleaner shop, G and S Group Service in Crouch End, North London, told me: "Grit in a carpet is like bits of glass. If it's trodden on, it cuts into the fibers."

A FIRST LOOK AT VACUUM CLEANERS

Ask your wife or partner where the vacuum is kept, and go and have a look at it right now, taking this book with you. Is it upright? If so, it is an upright vacuum cleaner. Is it on its belly? If so, it is a cylinder vacuum cleaner.

Uprights are the logical and slightly more expensive choice for the house that is largely carpeted. Get down and look at the business end of the thing. You might try turning it on. If you do that, you will see that it is equipped with a rolling brush. This agitates carpet fibers and loosens dirt before it is sucked up. It "beats as it sweeps as it cleans" to coin a phrase. Uprights are on wheels, with the point of suction set relatively high, so they move easily across a floor.

It used to be that if you had an upright, then you were stuck with the one vacuum/carpet interface. But for about the past thirty years they have usually come equipped with a hose and a variety of attachments. I associate uprights particularly with women. In clichéd musicals, the frustrated housewife waltzes with her upright vacuum cleaner while dreaming of her imaginary lover. In bad stage comedy, the housekeeper crassly interrupts delicately poised proceedings when she walks on with her upright vacuum blaring away. Or a barren marriage is signified by the way the husband reading the newspaper lifts his feet without needing to be told when his wife slides the upright beneath the sofa.

Cylinder vacuums are cheaper and more maneuverable. They are better for houses with a lot of hard floors, whether wood or stone—the rolling brushes of the uprights ought to be kept away from those for fear of scratching. (Some cylinder vacuums do come with attachments featuring rolling brushes.)

The other big distinction in the vacuum cleaner world is between those that collect the dust in paper bags, which need periodic changing, and bagless cleaners that collect the dust in a removable can.

If you have a bagless cleaner in your household, then you will probably know about it. You might even have been in on the purchase. A bagless cleaner is a statement. It's akin to having an Apple Mac or an electrical car. Like electrical cars they are perhaps more environmentally friendly in that you don't have to keep buying and throwing away the paper bags. Then again, where are you going to put the vacuumed-up dust when you empty out the can? Into a bag, I would suggest.

You also probably have to buy filters because most vacuum cleaners use these. When I mentioned to Brian of G and S Group Service that I proposed going into the question of filters, he said:

"I really wouldn't bother if I were you."

"Why not?"

"It's too complicated."

"But I have to address it in some way."

"Then tell people to talk to their dealer about it—and find out the cost of the filters before they buy the cleaner." If you think about it—which I never had done—then it's obvious that vacuum cleaners would need a filter. The air being drawn into the vacuum by the angled fan blades has to come out somewhere. It has to go through the dust-collecting paper bag, for example; otherwise, that bag would inflate and pop. The danger is that a percentage of the dust that has been vacuumed up will be released into the air along with this exhaust, and this is prevented by the filters.

"Some vacuums," said Brian, "have five filters, and they all have to be kept clean or changed regularly. That's how a lot of the manufacturers make their money: from selling the filters."

"Well, I knew about vacuum bags," I said, "but I never knew about filters."

He shrugged, as if to say that this was just the kind of ignorance he had to put up with.

"But how could I have been vacuuming for all these years and not known about filters?"

"You tell me," he said.

Seeing that I was depressed by the thought, Brian struck a brighter note: "Perhaps your wife knows about them?" he suggested.

I wondered. Had my wife been cleaning or replacing the filters on our cylinder vacuum for all of these years?

I went home and asked her.

"Did you know that vacuums have filters?"

"Vaguely."

"Have you ever replaced the filter on our vacuum?"

"Yes . . . yes, of course I have."

(I was impressed by this, because if I'd replaced the filter on the vacuum cleaner, I would certainly have mentioned it.)

"How many times?"

"No, wait . . . the filter, did you say? I've changed the *bag*. I don't like vacuum cleaners, you know that."

"Why not?'

"Because they're machines. That's why I never bother with them. Cleaning is about the relationship of your hands to your house."

The reason we were able to get away without knowing of the existence of vacuum cleaner filters was that we own a vacuum cleaner on which the filter—and in fact, everything else—is very hard wearing: a Henry. And in any discussion of men and vacuuming, the Henry merits special attention.

THE HENRY

The Henry is a sociologically interesting vacuum cleaner. It was launched in 1981 by a British company called Numatic, which is owned by a retiring individual always referred to by his publicity people as Mr. Duncan. The Henry is broadly classed as a cylinder vacuum cleaner, but it is not cylindrical. Strictly speaking, it is like a shop vac, and it has all the beauty and aerodynamic grace of a giant wart on wheels. It is red, and it has a face painted on it, hence the name.

Brian, of G and S Group Service, liked Henrys. "Good as gold, they are," he told me. "Strong suction, last forever."

The Henry is available in America but not widely, partly perhaps because Americans prefer upright vacuum cleaners. This is a shame, since if any vacuum cleaner is made for men, then the Henry is—and this by virtue of its robustness and simplicity. A handyman (note that last syllable) uses a picture of a Henry to advertise his services in a shop window near my house. A Henry is the only sort of vacuum cleaner you will see used by builders on building sites for what they confidently call "the final clean." (It would be an interesting sort of builder, incidentally, who used the newly available female counterpart to the Henry: the Hetty, which is pink and has mascara painted around the eyes.)

Numatic mainly makes industrial cleaning equipment, and the Henrys that are used in America are mainly used by industry rather than in the home. The sturdiness and bulk make the Henry look institutional, and you feel like a school janitor whenever you take it out of the closet. The filter is no delicate paper thing but a white cloth like a tea towel that rests above the dust bag. "It's extremely hard wearing," a company spokesman told me, "but you might want to clean it occasionally."

"How?"

"Oh, just put it into a carrier bag* and give it a bit of a bash."

The paper bags are sturdy and capacious. There is no indicator light on a Henry to alert you to the fact that the bag is full. You know it's full when the thing stops working (because suction is reduced on any vacuum when the dust receptacle is full).

The suction regulator is basically a hole in the topmost pipe, over which a bit of plastic can be slid. You leave the hole open for minimum suction, close it for maximum . . . as if anybody ever uses a Henry on less than maximum suction. The various Henrys come with particularly long electrical cords, and you wind them back in by turning a barrel with the satisfying, mixing motion of a man driving a tram in the 1930s.

----

* A polyethelene disposable bag of the sort given out in supermarkets.

BETTER VACUUMING

On the top of the standard cylinder vacuum cleaner attachment—the rectangular one about ten inches wide (the boring one)—there is usually a lever. Press it one way and something happens. Press it another way and something else happens. But the question is, what?

For years, I would press this lever back and forth, idly curious about what it did. And then one day I turned the attachment upside down and found out: the lever raises or lowers brushes. But that only begged another question: What are these brushes for?

They are for vacuuming hard surfaces, especially wooden floors, which should only be vacuumed with this attachment in this mode. You should also vacuum along the grain of the wood because that way, if you do scratch the wood (and you *are* going to), then you will be scratching it along the grain.

The crevice attachment, as previously noted, is good fun. As you're using it, you might come across, say, a pen that's dropped to the floor. No sooner do you think, *I'd better be careful of that pen*, than it's gone. (People ought really to have to pass a test before using the crevice attachment.) Try using it for getting all the fluff, single staples, and pins that get left in the corner of drawers. But the attachment that's the real dark horse of the vacuum stable is the upholstery brush attachment. Besides upholstery, you can clean venetian and cloth blinds, books, curtains, and lampshades with it, not that I ever do—we have lost our upholstery brush. But a lot of your dusting can be accomplished with this tool. It is the one that stops vacuuming from being floor bound. It gives the machine wings, so to speak.

The good news—from the idle man's point of view—is that upright vacuum cleaners glide easily, and there's no point pressing down hard when using the cylinder cleaners, because that blocks the flow of air. There is no virtue in vacuuming forcefully, in other words. But extra effort is rewarded in the sense that dirt will be removed in direct proportion to the number of repeated strokes across the same area. In vacuuming, unlike mopping, there is some point to repetition of cleaning strokes. The *Good Housekeeping* Web site recommends going over most areas at least three or four times, and seven times for "high-traffic" areas of the house. But for my own part, if I couldn't see any more dirt after one stroke, then I wouldn't do another six.

Oh, and you're really supposed to brush a carpet before you vacuum it. This raises up the fibers, clearing the way for the exit of the dirt.

VACUUMING STAIRS

I live in a bungalow, but as a boy I prided myself on my stair vacuuming. I'd go around the edges with a crevice tool, and then weigh in with the standard attachment. Yet I only ever did half the stairs, in that I ignored the risers, as the vertical sections are properly designated. I found out how to vacuum the risers by watching an instructional video on a Web site called Video Jug. In this, a woman appeared smiling at the foot of a staircase. There was a jump cut, and then she was wearing yellow rubber gloves and holding some vacuum cleaner attachments, at which point it was difficult to believe she wasn't going to do something sexual, but in fact, she proceeded to vacuum the stairs, employing the basic method described above. The revelation came when she addressed the stair risers, which she vacuumed with the standard attachment reversed, so that its back edge faced forward on the end of the vacuum pipe. That way, it was at the right angle to meet the riser.

Incidentally, do not balance a cylinder vacuum cleaner on a high stair while you yourself are standing on a higher one. You might get away with this for a while, but one day—when you are feeling particularly short of money—the cleaner will tumble down the stairs and never work again. Always stand below the vacuum cleaner, where you can arrest its fall.

WHAT NOT TO VACUUM

In her incredibly enormous book, *Home Comforts*, Cheryl Mendelson advises, "When vacuuming delicate upholstery and antiques, set the suction level of the vacuum on low. If necessary, further protect them by covering them with a nylon or plastic screen and vacuum through the screen with the upholstery nozzle." In the case of men, that advice needs refining as follows: do not vacuum delicate upholstery and antiques.

And do not vacuum up liquid. There are vacuum cleaners designed to take water as well as dust. Yours is probably not one. "You'll most likely jigger the engine," said Brian of G and S Group Service with characteristic ruefulness, "and you will certainly dissolve the bag."

Do not vacuum your computer keyboard. I sucked the End key off mine.

Dust

WHY DUST?

My stepmother told me that she wakes up on a fine day with mixed feelings. "Because when it's sunny, you can see all the dust." This reminded me of something I'd read concerning the introduction of electric lighting into homes. It too illuminated dust, making more work for millions of women, whether housewives or domestic servants.

Was the difference between my stepmother's reaction to a sunny day and mine the difference between men and women, or just the difference between her and me? How many men run a finger over an out-of-the-way surface to see how much dust is there? My wife does it in every hotel room we check into, and if the finger comes back dusty, I know we are not going to enjoy our holiday. Like Sherlock Holmes, she can diagnose everything from that one small sample: the hotel is not properly cleaned; therefore, it is not properly run; the staff will probably be mentally inadequate. And, of course, she's usually right.

I like the word "dust." The stuff looks nice swirling in a sunbeam, and I used to think there was a kind of peacefulness about dust, like gray grass. Its presence signified an unneurotic approach to life. In Charles Dickens's novel *Our Mutual Friend*, Mr. Boffin, the Golden Dustman, a person of "great moral straightness" for all his shambolic appearance, keeps mountains of the stuff in his front garden. It is the agency of magic in *Peter Pan*, and in Philip Pullman's His Dark Materials series. Dust is, in a sense, only us, and so we ought to be at ease around it. We are, as Hamlet says, "the quintessence of dust."

Dust is indeed mainly human skin cells. But it also comes with its own parasite: the dust mites that feed on those cells. Any man who saw a dust mite under a microscope might at least think about doing some dusting. He might then imagine himself to be conducting a massacre rather than just camping about with some feathers on a stick.

Dust mites, which are related to spiders and scorpions and look uglier than both, live on the falling scales of our skins and other organic material, and we breathe in their corpses, their enzymes, and their excreta. Dust mites do kill, in the sense that they, and their bits and pieces, are one of many allergens in dust that can cause asthma attacks.

Dust, cats, and pollen are the biggest causes of asthma attacks, the numbers of which are rising fast, partly because the overheated or air-conditioned rooms we live in are not properly aired. Fresh air dilutes dust, and ultraviolet rays are thought to kill dust mites. In this sense, the house itself is one of the great enemies of housework, as people used to be better at recognizing. In suburban York on the hot summer days of my childhood, women would lay out sheets and cushion covers, even mattresses and sofas, in the front garden, just as though they were done with housework forever and meant to sell off all the articles that tied them to it. But really they were just giving the living room an airing.

The practice of airing mattresses was commended to me by a small, intelligent, earnest man called Henry, who'd put a leaflet through our door introducing himself as "The Mattress Doctor." Henry and the thirty or so other mattress doctors in Britain—it's a franchise—will remove dust mites and dust in general from the insides of mattresses using a very powerful vacuum cleaner that also vibrates the mattress. The "doctors" then treat the mattresses with ultraviolet light, which, as Henry explained, "dust mites hate . . . because it kills them."

My wife and I sleep on twin mattresses, and Henry

began by doing a test with his vacuum on my mattress. (Incidentally, to clarify any confusion that might arise from a reading of the previous chapter, this man was called Henry; his vacuum cleaner was not.) He collected the dust onto a black cloth filter and showed me the result after fifteen seconds of vacuuming: there was about half an eggcupful of dust.

He explained that the average double bed harbors 2 million dust mites. The sample from my half of the bed was, he said, about average. "So only about a million dust mites?" I said. Henry nodded and as he set to work with the full treatment, we talked dust mites for a while, and it seemed that there really was very little good to be said for them. "You can get five on a pinhead," he said, "although of course you won't see them, which is why lots of people don't bother about them, even though [the mites] might be making them ill. It's the droppings that really trigger the allergic reactions, and they excrete about twenty droppings a day." Approximately 80 percent of dust mites in a house are in the bedroom. That's where we shed most of our skin, and dust mites thrive in the heat and humidity of a bed.

Henry explained that we are all fighting on two fronts, assuming we are fighting at all: against the dust mites themselves and the allergens they generate. For example: a hot wash is needed to kill dust mites in bedding, whereas a cool one will deal with the allergens. Dry-cleaning kills the allergens but not the mites. Dusting will help deal with both (and we will come to that in a minute).

Mattress doctoring is a growth industry partly because ordinary vacuum cleaners will only suck the dust off the surface of the mattress. The old-fashioned way of cleaning the interior of the mattress was to take it out into the garden and beat it, but if you tried to do that with a modern, structured mattress . . . well, it would probably hit you back. In any case, modern mattresses are too heavy to be carted about by one person. (If this were not the case, then the sleeping arrangements in many homes would be subject to much more frequent alteration and many marriages would either end sooner or last longer.) The other thing keeping the mattress doctors busy is dust allergy, and my eldest son is a sufferer. I would have asked Henry to vacuum his mattress had we not just bought him a brand-new one and wrapped it in a dust-proof cover.

A dust allergy ought to dictate a certain style of interior décor: a severe, Trappist minimalism. The worth of your every possession ought to be balanced against the amount of dust it harbors.

But try telling that to my son. The doctor—our general practitioner, I mean, not the mattress doctor—asked whether the boy's bedroom was cluttered, and I pictured it as he spoke. My son is technically minded, and his room at the time contained the following: two computers with attachments such as microphones for voice activation, printers, and scanners; two typewriters ("in case the computers break down"); a wide-screen television (but not flatscreen; this mother is wide in both directions); an eight-millimeter cine projector; a night-vision finder (or something like that); a bike; a collection of trunks, crates, and boxes containing old books and comics; one of the untidiest desks in England (I should think); two sofas; a wicker chair; two chests of drawers; a trestle table retrieved from the recycling center; a record player with amplifier and quadraphonic sound (i.e., four dust-covered speakers); a couple of beat boxes; and a biggish and dusty radio.

One American author advises consulting a child psychologist before altering the habitat of your dust-allergic child, but I only came across that passage some weeks after I'd marched into my son's room and said, "Right, we're getting rid of all this crap."

We had a clear-out. We began a policy of more regular dusting and cleaning the (wooden) floor with a damp cloth; we enclosed his mattress in a dust protector and bought allergen-resistant pillowcases. We tried to keep the blinds up and the window open for longer—and I think my son's condition did improve.

It was the beginning of my interest in dust. Once I saw that dust was actually malicious, the removal of it became a more noble endeavor. And dusting would lessen my feelings of guilt about the two or three cigars I smoke in my study every week, since nicotine latches on to dust, prolonging its presence in the house.

DURING DUSTING, WHERE DOES THE DUST GO?

If you flick the duster about, the dust will rise into the air and, as you step through to another room to savor a job well done over a cup of tea, it will gradually settle back down into roughly the place it occupied before you applied yourself to it. To seriously disturb dust is to do more harm than good. The trick is to gather the dust up into the duster, to retain the dust on the duster, and to keep turning the duster over so that you are always using a clean side of it. It helps if the duster is slightly damp. When the duster is completely covered in dust, I'm afraid that you have to start using another one. Yes, you must have more than one duster, and an old copy of *Good Housekeeping* that I read suggested dusting with a duster in either hand.

If you're going to buy a feather duster—and that's probably a big "if" in the case of most men—then don't buy a synthetic one, of the sort waved about on stage by Ken Dodd. "They might just do for reaching down behind the radiator," the man in the cleaning shop said dismissively. Otherwise, he told me, they just scatter the dust about. Instead, he recommended an ostrich feather duster. "Ostrich feathers carry an electrostatic charge that enables them to collect up dust," he said, which seemed an evolutionary error. I mean, why would an ostrich want dusty feathers? But I was willing to take his word for it. Certainly, ostrich feather dusters are impressively expensive, and they were given out as prizes by Anthea Turner on a BBC television program called *Perfect Housewife*, if that's any recommendation.*

In the field of conventional cloth dusters, the man at the cleaning shop recommended those made of microfiber. These are a polyester-nylon mix with tiny hairs that stand up. "Microfiber is often called the miracle material," the label on Scotch-Brite Multi-Purpose Cleaning Cloths modestly declares. I don't know about miraculous, but I would agree that a microfiber duster retains more dust than a cotton one—probably to the degree to which a microfiber duster is more expensive than a cotton duster. In fact, its properties of retention are such that you have to be careful in case it becomes abrasive.

DUSTING THINGS THAT ARE HARD TO DUST

Dusting your books can be a fiddly operation. "The best way to dust books," the estimable Rachel Simhon severely remarks in her very useful volume, *The Housewife's Handbook*, "is to read them." In *Classic Household Hints*, Susan Waggoner suggests dusting books with a paintbrush two or three inches wide. She also contends that "stubborn

---

* Anthea ran a "remedial school" for "less than perfect" housewives. For example: "Anthea takes on a mother of four, and a hairdresser with horrendous hoarding habits."

dust caught in the crevices of artificial flowers and porce-lain figurines can be removed with a small watercolour brush," which I should imagine will be a matter of purely academic interest to most readers of this book.

And don't climb stepladders and lean out precariously in order to dust high shelves, because that's just another way the dust mites have of killing us all.

7

Cleaning

AREN'T MEN *SUPPOSED* TO BE DIRTY?

Men and dirt do seem to go together. Feminists reject the biblical association of female cleanliness with sexual virtue, but the first words they use of any man guilty of some sexual impropriety are *smutty*, *grubby*, and *filthy*.

Of course men do the same back, but often with a small, and admittedly conditional, note of approval. Look at the back of a grimy white van: instead of cleaning it, one man has written: "I wish my wife was this dirty," while another has responded: "She is!" These men are like two boys making mud pies. Not that boys ever do make mud pies anymore, a fact that is very much regretted. Men worry that their sons are not getting dirty enough, owing to spending too much time at the computer screen and not enough being Just William, frolicking in the fields with vegetation in their hair. I myself have lamented this in print, comparing my own boyhood in semirural York with that of my sons in London. Every night in summer, I'd come home from the fields around York—those fields that are now the A1237—and stand impassively on the doorstep, like a dog being groomed, as my mother brushed me down and picked the larger twigs out of my sweater while exclaiming, "I don't know . . . you come home black bright!" But her tone was one of affectionate exasperation rather than anger. She didn't want me to be one of the pallid, strange, well-presented boys like Walter-the-Softie in the comic *The Beano*, who wore a bow tie, and walked down the street with straight lines radiating from him to indicate his extreme cleanness. (That was until Dennis the Menace got to him.)

I believe that my mother would have assumed that males were naturally dirty and females were naturally clean. In 1974, in her book *Housewife*, Ann Oakley asked how many women were ever seen with greasy and neglected hair, as compared to the numbers of men happy to look like that. It's still a good question in 2008, when every newsagent has a shelf full of magazines—women's magazines—making money out of showing female celebrities looking scruffy.

But any man seeking to exploit this discrepancy should

take care. In Victorian times there was some nobility in being an industrial worker caked in soot, but these men had an excuse, and in any case, they invariably prided themselves on their cleanliness come Sunday. Even today there might be some charm in being rumpled and distracted, but not in being filthy, and certaainly not after a certain age. The young boy indulged in his making of mud pies had better not turn into a dirty old man, and if the only thing keeping him from being one is his wife or partner—if she is, in fact, his cleaner, like the tickbird that stands on the shoulders of the hippopotamus, picking off the insects—then that's almost as bad.

A FIRST LOOK INTO THE CLEANING CUPBOARD

The first time that I had a proper look inside the cupboard in which my wife keeps our household cleaning fluids, which was about ten years after I'd married her, I was appalled by the number of bottles and sprays:* Waitrose Power Kitchen Cleaner, Brasso, Shampoo 1001 for Carpets and Upholstery, Troubleshooter 1001 for Carpets and Upholstery, Tesco Antibacterial Eucalyptus (tremendously enigmatic, that one, until I looked at the words *washing-up liquid* in tiny letters on the label), Sainsbury's Bathroom

---

* What follows are the names of mainly British cleaning products, and those names were as unfamiliar to me as they would be to most Americans.

Cleaner, Mr Muscle ("Loves the jobs you hate"), Easy Care Maintenance Product (this one remained enigmatic, despite lengthy scrutiny), Lavender Furniture Polish (with Beeswax) . . . and that was only about half of them.

I decided that the manly thing would be to get this lot down to one or at the most two. And I imagined myself as going about the house wearing these on a belt, in holsters, ready for anything.

I would try to find a universal cleaner. If I knew that I had something that cleaned everything, then I'd be much more *likely* to clean everything.

I went off to my local hardware shop, which has a couple of long shelves full of cleaning fluids. (It's better for a man to buy cleaning agents from a hardware shop—it makes cleaning seem akin to the banging-in of nails and other respectable pursuits.) Again, I was numbed by the variety and by the stridency of the hype.

The essence of the claims made on the labels was encapsulated in the name of a product called simply Miracle Foam ("Cleans as It Clings to Vertical and Horizontal Surfaces"). Perhaps a certain dark humor was being employed here. This was certainly the case with something called Bath Power (slogan: "This Product Actually Works"). Discounting such ferocious specialists as Shower Shine, Mildew and Mould, Bathbrite, or 100% Limescale Destroyer, I hunted for all-rounders. . . .

It seemed that many of the bottles presented themselves as either bathroom or kitchen cleaners, but then my eye fell on Flash Multi-Surface: "Superb cleaning everywhere." Well, I couldn't go wrong with that, but next to it was Flash Multi-Surface and Glass, so that went one better, because it not only cleaned everything, it also cleaned *glass*. That did seem to be a bonus because I began to see that a lot of the multipurpose cleaners balked at glass in general and especially windows. There also seemed to be a general trepidation about painted or varnished surfaces, and in spite of its claims of universality of application, Flash Multi-Surface and Glass shared these: "On painted surfaces, try on a small, inconspicuous place before using."

I then spotted Flash All Purpose Cleaner. Surely "All Purpose" was an advance on "Multi-Surface," in the sense that it might be able to clean things that didn't have a surface. It was cheaper as well (possibly because it didn't have a spray top) and was based on impressive-sounding "Rhodia's Surf S Technology." It was for cleaning "hard surfaces," but again there was the reservation about painted and varnished ones: "Use dilute. If in doubt test on a hidden area before use."

I then began to realize that some of the cleaners had antibacterial properties. I had forgotten about bacteria. Perhaps I would need a whole lot of other products to deal with them. My eye fell on Dettol Antibacterial Surface Cleanser, which promised to kill 99.9 percent of bacteria and viruses. But I recalled from the television adverts of my youth that Domestos killed "*all* known germs"—and in fact it still does, or still says it does, for the boast was on the label of a Domestos bottle not far from the Dettol range. Then again, I knew Domestos was bleach, and I was aware that people had reservations about bleach, and that a boy I was at school with—an idiot, admittedly—had nearly died after drinking half a cupful of it. In any case, 99.9 percent seemed a pretty good strike rate. I would be happy to settle for that. I'd have to be very unlucky for it to be plagued by the 0.1 percent of bacteria and viruses that Dettol Antibacterial Surface Cleanser was powerless to defeat.

I next saw a whole shelf full of products for cleaning toilets, and some others especially for limescale, whatever that was. This was getting out of hand. I would develop a more focused approach to cleaning products by means of hard research, or at least by talking to someone who'd done some hard research. But this aspiration, as it turned out, was naïve. In twenty years of interviewing people as a journalist, I have never come upon a harder task than pinning somebody down about cleaning products.

I began with my wife.

"What do you know about cleaning products?" I asked her one night at about eleven o'clock.

"Oh God," she said.

She was reading a novel by Georgette Heyer—female escapism of the eighteenth-century, sub–Jane Austen kind. Those books are all about significant sidelong glances over candlelit dinners. No wonder she didn't want to talk to me about cleaning products.

"Do you know what I think?" I said. "I think there are too many cleaning products."

"When I first left home," my wife said, not looking up from her book, "I did almost all my cleaning with one product."

"What was that?"

"Jif," she said simply.*

"I've heard of that. . . . I think I once cleaned something with it."

"It's a cream cleaner. I like cream cleaners."**

"Why?"

"It's just an attractive way of . . . incorporating all the chemicals, I suppose. It's mainly sprays that you get now. I don't think Jif exists anymore," she added, turning the page of her book. In fact, it does, in a way. . . .

Jif underwent a similar depressing process to the one that turned plain-speaking Marathon chocolate bar into creepy and incomprehensible Snickers. The name Snickers is presumably not quite as ludicrous in some languages as it is here. (I picture the marketing meeting: "I warn you," says one executive, "in Britain this is going to look

---

* She was not referring to the American peanut butter brand of the same name.

** But they are out of fashion, especially in America. The trouble is that you can't spray a cream cleaner. They are slow, in other words.

like knickers with an 'S' on the front." "That's too bad," says another. "We've got to press ahead with international brand harmonization.") I read on the Internet that Jif had been known as Cif across the world but the manufacturer, Unilever, held off from calling it Cif in Britain for fear that it would remind people of the word *syphilis*, which it does, as soon as the fact is mentioned. But once again the principle of brand harmonization triumphed over mere comprehensibility, and Jif became Cif in Britain.

In view of my wife's affection for Jif/Cif, I called Unilever to see if I could speak to somebody about it. I left three messages but received no answer. And so began many weeks of frustration. The people who knew the science of cleaning either (a) were too busy to speak to me (there is no more harassed class of person in Britain, I have concluded, than microbiologists—there must not be enough of them to go around) or (b) reacted with amused amazement, when, after listening to some unintelligible speech on chemistry, I asked, "But what's the application of that to cleaning the sink?"

With a few honorable exceptions, the people from the cleaning industry either did not return my calls or answered with such wariness—apparently fearing that I was trying to lure them into a trap with questions such as, "Which of your products is best suited to cleaning the bath?"—that the response would become unquotable.

The UK Cleaning Products Industry Association would not speak to me on the grounds that anything they said might be prejudicial to any one or more of their members. As for the women of my acquaintance, they seemed rather ashamed of speaking about cleaning, either (I couldn't quite work it out) because it is the most demeaning aspect of domestic work, or because they didn't know as much about it as they thought they should.

If you want to silence a woman, ask her about cleaning. There is almost as much of a stigma attached to the woman who demonstrates a knowledge of cleaning as there is to the man who does. It is the most relentless of domestic tasks and the most humiliating, being performed in a supplicatory posture, and, necessarily, amid dirt. In the days of the *Upstairs, Downstairs* world, male servants did not as a rule do any cleaning apart from that of shoes and silver.

The implication of knowing about cleaning is that you don't know about anything else and yet, as noted above, the *unclean* woman has long been vilified for a laxity that is taken to be essentially sexual. Where domestic cleaning was concerned, I seemed to detect a sullen standoff: the housewives against the scientists, with the marketing men muddying the waters in the middle. The reticence of the makers of cleaning products is down to the need— as they see it—to maintain commercial confidentiality in a cutthroat market; that of the women is explained by embarrassment.

I tried to get people talking, and have assembled some very basic principles on the art of cleaning, the first of which was commended to me by Mr. Colin Hasson, press officer and lifetime vice president of the British Institute of Cleaning Science, an educational organization for the cleaning industry: "Read the instructions. It's amazing how many people don't. In fact, that's almost the number-one problem we have in the cleaning industry." I said I would tell my readers to do that. "Of course," Mr. Hasson added gloomily, "six percent of the country can't read at all, so you're never going to be able to tell *them*."

This chapter will not make you an expert on cleaning, but then I'm not sure that anybody is an expert, and I feel fairly confident in saying that it will bring you up to the standard of most women.

A DAY-OLD HOUSEHOLD CLOTH CONTAINS OVER 30 TRILLION COLONIES OF BACTERIA. IS THIS A PROBLEM?

Our sense of imminent catastrophe was put down to millennial anxiety in the late 1990s, but it is still with us, and germs are at the top of the list of modern demons, along with feral youths, Osama bin Laden, and falling house prices. Look at the labels on the cleaning products: "Dettol kills E. coli, salmonella, MRSA, Listeria, Rotavirus," and so on. A recent ad for dishwashers read: "Germs multiply at an alarming rate. A day-old dishcloth or used kitchen towel contains thirty trillion colonies of bacteria." (That *is* a lot, isn't it? But then again, they're very small.)

The people on the front line of the fight against germs are the ones likely to be sued, or at least sacked, over any lapse in hygiene. That is why there are toilets in motorway service stations that have two plastic faces positioned near the exits. You press the smiley face if you found the toilets to be in a satisfactory condition, the scowling one if not. (I always press the scowling face as a matter of principle.)

But we are all becoming more germ conscious, and a counterreaction has developed. The "hygiene hypothesis," which emerged in the late 1980s, suggested that the rising number of allergies diagnosed in society might be connected to our increasingly hygienic living conditions. In a nutshell, this says that our immune systems need bacteria as a boxer needs a sparring partner. Then again, salmonella and E. coli are real. Professor Sally Bloomfield of the International Scientific Forum on Home Hygiene has written, "Although there is good evidence that microbial exposure in early childhood can protect against allergies, there is no evidence that we need exposure to harmful microbes or that we need to suffer a clinical infection."

I think I am going to risk saying that we need a balanced approach. In her book *The Dirt on Clean: An Unsanitized History,* the American author Katherine Ashenburg quotes Tore Midtvedt, a Swedish microbiologist and an advocate of an end to "the war on germs," as follows: "I'm not saying that we should be more dirty. I'm saying we should be less clean." I commend that remark to my readers. When the question of why you have not cleaned the kitchen floor next comes up, it ought to mollify—or at least temporarily baffle—your irate wife or partner.

By cleaning you remove germs; by using a disinfectant you kill them . . . dead, as the ads tautologically have it. There's no point disinfecting without first cleaning. Cleaning ought to involve warm water and soap or detergents. A detergent—Flash, for example—is a cleansing agent, like soap. But unlike soap, which is mainly fat, a detergent is mainly synthetic. (Detergents were developed during the Second World War, when we were running out of soap.) Most people settle, most of the time, for removing germs rather than killing them, and many experts would say that this was okay. In fact, it strikes me that a paradox of cleaning science is that the people who know the most about it seem to keep invoking the benefits of hot soapy water.

However, you wouldn't be removing those germs if you kept using the same dirty cloth. Writing in the *Daily Mail*, Professor Charles Penn, a microbiologist, revealed a fairly relaxed approach to kitchen germs: "While I am careful in the kitchen about keeping implements and cloths clean, there's nothing sophisticated in my approach—I just wash them in hot soapy water and leave them to dry. And once or twice a week I soak them for an hour in bleach."

I myself consider any use of bleach to be quite sophisticated, as I will explain further below. If I am going to disinfect, then I would usually use Dettol, partly because the little sword on the label always reminds me of cocktails. It is an "antiseptic disinfectant": you get the two products for the price of one, and I reason that if it is good enough for the cut on my finger, then it's good enough for my bathroom floor. Bleach I certainly would not put on the cut on my finger. Bleach is a strong, chemically simple and cheap disinfectant (and whitener of clothes). But it's, like, scary, man. You've got to know what you're doing with bleach. Mix chlorine bleach (the most common type) with the wrong chemical and it can blow up. I've never actually heard of this happening to anyone, but correct use of bleach perhaps requires more concentration than most of the readers of this book will want to bring to housework, and so nothing more will be said about it.

You might regard your disinfectant, of whatever sort, as an emergency recourse, like the fire extinguisher. You will bring it into play if someone has urinated all over the floor (if you have perfectly normal young boys, in other words), if someone has thrown up, or if you've made a bit of a mess with raw meat, raw chicken especially.

Incidentally, be careful about disinfecting a surface on which food is prepared. You need a "food-safe" disinfectant for that. The sprays that employees in cafés and bars piously wield when clearing tables are sanitizers, which combine a detergent element with a food-safe germ killer. They claim to be able to clean and disinfect at once, in other words. A "food safe," natural, and charmingly "retro" way to disinfect a wooden chopping board would be to do what the eighteenth-century surgeons did with their wooden operating tables: scrub it with salt (but see also How to Impress People with Bicarbonate of Soda).

I'VE BEEN THINKING OF CLEANING THE BATH. . . .

A press release sent to me for a bathroom cleaning product began: "With the average person spending up to eighteen months of their life in the bathroom, it's no wonder we want somewhere to relax and unwind after a hard day's work."

Now there's something a bit wrong with that sentence, it seems to me. But people certainly do bathe more regularly than they used to, and so the old-fashioned greasy gray tidemark is not so often encountered.

When I was a boy, I had a bath only on Wednesdays and Sundays, and my sister and my father shared the same water. My dad's motto—bred into him by wartime austerity—was "Leave that bath in," whereas my habitual countercry was "Can I have the first bath?" Whoever had the last bath really had drawn the short straw: not only did you emerge from the water dirtier than when you went in, but you also had to clean the bath, and the equipment on hand for the job was scouring powder and a scouring sponge.

Scouring is the oldest form of domestic cleaning, and the vigorous scouring of baths went the way of smoking in the house, telling Irish jokes, and hitting your children. I recall the enormous, frightening baths, scarred by scouring, that I used to lie in during the two hours a day when hot water was available in the boardinghouses of Blackpool. And I remember when the turning point came: an ad of the mid-1970s in which a shrewd-looking Scottish woman in a housecoat lectured a naïve young skivvy: "Flash cleans baths without scratching."

This is all to do with the material from which the bath is made. Many modern baths, especially the cheaper or more exotically shaped ones, are made of vinyl. (Rap on your bath with your knuckles: if it doesn't ring, it might well be vinyl.) These are not strong. I was once contemplating buying a vinyl bath, and the salesman warned me that I must not drop heavy articles into it. I asked him, "What heavy article might you be likely to be carrying when you're anywhere near the bath?'

"The soap dish," he replied, instantly and irrefutably.

Vinyl baths also do not take to being scoured. Try it, and you might put a hole in them. Most other baths are steel, covered in vitreous enamel, and hard scouring will remove the enamel. You could theoretically have a steel bath re-enameled, but the worth of the bath would not justify the cost, whereas it *would* be worth re-enameling an iron bath of the expensive kind that you still might see standing on lion's feet in a country house hotel.

After those early, scouring days, I went twenty years without once cleaning a bath, and when I first got married I noticed there were no bath-cleaning potions or utensils anywhere near the bath in any case. So I carried on not cleaning the bath. I suppose I was vaguely—and slightly guiltily—aware that the bath was always clean when I got into it. But you don't look a gift horse in the mouth, and I went on having my two baths a day (having a bath is a sort of hobby of mine), always washing my face with the black face flannel* my wife kept near the soap dish.

One day I happened to return to the bathroom shortly after having bathed, and there was my wife, squirting shampoo onto the face flannel. I looked on appalled as she stooped down and began rubbing it over the side of the bath as the last of the water drained away.

"Hold on," I said, "I clean my face with that."

She wasn't very sympathetic. She rather took the view that, in not having been alerted to the true use of the flannel, I was being justly punished for never enquiring as to the whereabouts of any bath-cleaning materials. She explained that she did not want her bath-cleaning kit near the bath because it looked ugly. I told her that I could hardly believe that a quick wipe with shampoo

---

* What you call a washcloth, we call a face flannel.

and face flannel would get the job done properly, and she said, "So you've gone from not cleaning the bath at all to wanting to do it to the highest standards?"

"That is exactly the position," I said, and from that moment, I took over the cleaning of the bath, and what is more, I carried on doing it for about three weeks.

It's quite easy, really. You don't need separate kitchen and bathroom cleaners. Take your Flash All Purpose, say, or, if you prefer, Flash Multi-Surface; wipe it around on a cloth (and you might as well do the sink and the shower screen at the same time).

If you shave in the bath, it helps to splash water against the sides as the water is running out—this in order to remove any bristles and shaving soap that would otherwise be left there. (One woman we know admitted that she cleans the bath as she lies in it. "That's because she's Catholic," my wife later told me.)

You might then mop the bathroom floor with warm water and a dash of liquid soap. You may also feel the need to go over the bathroom floor with dilute disinfectant if you have a young child—a young boy especially.

If a young boy is really concentrating, then as much as 80 percent of his wee might find its way into the toilet bowl. If he is talking as he micturates—as in yelling at his brother, "No, you can't have a go on my PlayStation! Leave it alone!"—then the figure goes down to about 50 percent, because young boys can't talk and urinate at the same time. In *The Mum's Book (For the Mum Who's Best at*

Everything), Alison Maloney suggests putting a Ping-Pong ball in the toilet and telling the boy to make a game of aiming at it. Apparently, it will not flush away. But it's too late for my own sons, who are now approaching my own rate of accuracy: a steady 95 percent or so.

TOILET CLEANING: AN OVERVIEW

There's a kind of reverse glamour about cleaning the toilet. Since your expectation of enjoying the job will be set at absolute zero, it will be quite hard to be disappointed. Most of the manuals will tell you to wear rubber gloves when about the job, and possibly goggles as well, to avoid splashback from whatever's in the toilet already, and also from what you put into it. One Web site recommends using a small mirror for looking under the toilet rim, and "fluorescent-type black light" for detecting urine, which "fluoresces a dull yellow under this black light." You're not going in there with mild green Fairy Liquid* and a song on your lips, in other words; this is an all-out assault on germ HQ. Or so I'd always regarded it.

But when I spoke to Dr. Val Curtis, director of the Hygiene Centre at the London School of Hygiene and Tropi-

---

* The most famous brand of dishwashing liquid in Britain; prides itself on its gentleness. Its manufacturers deterred many British men from doing the washing up (not that they really needed deterring) by the slogan: "Hands that do dishes can be soft as your face."

cal Medicine, she struck a subtly different note. "By all means go ahead, if you want to throw some bleach or disinfectant down there. It'll make your toilet look and smell nice and people won't say bad things about you."

"But you seem very laid-back about it," I said. "Surely it's essential to disinfect the toilet, say, once a week?"

"Well, then, what about the other days of the week?" she replied, amused.

Dr. Curtis is of the soap-and-hot-water school. She believes that disinfecting in the home is not, as a rule, essential: "Yes, the toilet is one of your critical points. One gram of feces contains more bacteria than there are people on the planet. But the point is to clean."

"To clean rather than disinfect?"

"By all means disinfect, but yes."

And the particular priority is to keep what we might bluntly call shit away from what we might, equally frankly, call our hands. If Dr. Curtis has one parting message for the readers of this book, it's that old favorite: "Wash your hands after going to the toilet."

This means that the toilet *handle* becomes a more suitable candidate for disinfection than the toilet bowl, and you wouldn't want to do that with most of the products designed specifically for cleaning the toilet bowls, because you are advised to keep these away from your skin. Instead, you might want to use an antiseptic disinfectant.

Toilet cleaners, incidentally, stand out on the shelves

by virtue of their crooked necks, which invite you to spray them under the rim. Most of them claim to disinfect, clean, and remove limescale. I go for something blue, in memory of the days of Mrs. Buffard.

INTO THE KITCHEN

Once you've done the bathroom, pick up your Flash Multi-Purpose (or whatever), your bucket, your liquid soap and disinfectant (if using), and trudge through into the kitchen. I mean, there's no point in putting it all away and then getting it out again.

But there are also some kitchen specialisms you may need to master. There may well be a lot of stainless steel in your kitchen, for example. This has been fashionable since the 1980s, and gives you kitchen the charm of . . . well, of an operating theater, or perhaps an abattoir. My wife bought a stainless-steel fridge-freezer and then a stainless-steel microwave to match. Later, we bought a stainless-steel bread bin and toaster to match the microwave and the fridge. The more stainless steel you have, the more stainless steel you will get.

Stainless steel is so called because it doesn't rust rather than—as might have been more honest—because it doesn't stain. While stainless steel is hygienic and quite easy to clean, it can be marked by dirty water, hard water, acidic foods, and table salt, among other substances.

You should be aware of what kind of stainless steel you're dealing with. Generally, it can be cleaned with a damp cloth, or a cloth with a mild detergent on it, in which case you should wipe off the detergent with water. Then buff up the surface with a soft, dry cloth.

You can buy proprietary stainless-steel cleaners, but they are not easy to find. We polish our fridge with a microfiber mitten, or "mitt," as you are supposed to call it. Well, I say "we" polish our fridge . . . I have done it once. When I used the mitt, I found it worked better if I spat on it. Later, I looked up the instructions and discovered that you're supposed to dampen one side of the mitten for the initial clean, and then buff with the other, so I was sort of right.

THE BIG ONE: CLEANING THE OVEN

You lift your fish pie from the oven and a few droplets of white sauce spill out, but that's fine. It has been cooked "until the sauce is bubbling," as directed by Delia.* But in a few weeks, or—more likely—a few months' time,

---

* Delia Smith, that is, Britain's most famous, and richest, cook, and the author of numerous homely cookbooks. I associate her with comfort food, and the dishes singled out for mention on the back cover of her *Complete Cookery Course* are flaky fish pie, Christmas pudding, and crunchy roast potatoes. In discussion of British domesticity she is inescapable and will crop up again later in this book.

you're going to be desperately scraping away at those droplets and roaring, "What the hell *is* this stuff? It's like black bloody concrete." Yes, you ought to be mopping up every oven spillage as it happens, before the stuff sets, because the big oven clean is one of the most daunting household jobs. I would rather do my tax return than clean the oven; I would rather . . . well, I believe I would rather put a duvet into a duvet cover than do it.

Part of the trouble is that there seems to be an infinite amount of dirt in there. Whatever cleaner you use, your sponge or cloth always comes up black. Eventually, you just have to stop. But before you can stop, you've got to start.

Make sure you've got the radio tuned to something good, because you're going to be at it for anything up to an hour, and you're not going to be able to touch anything but the inside of the oven during that time. You could begin by steaming away some of the caked-on grease by putting a roasting tin full of boiling water and lemon halves into the oven for a while. That's all very natural and organic, but then you're probably going to want to put on your rubber gloves before turning to your extremely toxic, if-swallowed-write-your-will, contains-Christ-knows-what-but-gets-the-job-done proprietary oven cleaner.

Or then again . . .

The firm called Ecover, whose products you might have noticed becoming more widely available of late, do not make an oven cleaner as such but recommend their cream cleaner for the job.

This company is the longest-established maker of ecological cleaning products. They are manufactured from renewable plant extracts, and sustainable minerals at a factory in Belgium with grass growing on the roof (this is deliberate: it has been planted there). Clare Allman, the marketing manager of Ecover UK, told me, "Our sales are very definitely on an upward curve. People are increasingly concerned that petrochemical cleaning products never biodegrade."

The firm started by making a washing powder without phosphates and then branched out into cleaning products. They do not make a disinfectant. "Normal domestic cleaning," says Ms. Allman, "is not about disinfecting. It is about removing the dirt where the germs grow."

She believes that men are more likely to be interested in ecological cleaning than women. "But they don't buy the products, so there's a discrepancy there."

I gave her my theory about why men might be more ecological in their housework, and it was tied in with something Colin Hasson of the British Institute of Cleaning Science had told me: "You can now do a university degree in cleaning, but we could only sell it to the university chancellors by calling it 'environmental cleaning.'"

Self-importance, in other words, is probably just as important here as ethical considerations: a man doesn't just want to clean the bath; he wants to clean the bath and tell himself he's saving the planet.

HOW TO IMPRESS PEOPLE WITH BICARBONATE OF SODA

Bicarbonate of soda (a.k.a. baking soda) can be used as a rising agent for cakes, as you may already be dimly aware. But it can also be used for cleaning your teeth (and was regularly so used a hundred years ago, perhaps in conjunction with attar of roses, precipitated chalk, borax, and powdered orris root—try it for the authentic, salty taste of Edwardian England), for making mushy peas, for cleaning beer off a carpet, for powering a model rocket made of a plastic camera-film canister (my eldest son has often burnt our lawn doing this), for reducing the acidity of stewed fruit, as a cure for spots, to ease the pain of bee—though not wasp—stings, as a base in the production of crack cocaine, as a general household cleaning agent . . . and I would certainly like to meet the man who has used it for all of these purposes.

If a cure for global warming is ever found, then it will probably turn out to involve bicarbonate of soda. Meanwhile, they recently cleaned the Statue of Liberty with it. This mild alkali is certainly getting a very good press at the moment, there being a mood in favor of simple, biodegradable cleaning products.

As a domestic aid, it is more or less infinitely useful. Bicarbonate of soda can be used to soften water, fight grease, and neutralize odors. Mixed into a paste with water, it becomes very mildly abrasive. It can be used to clean the painted surfaces that the powerful detergents are wary of, or the insides of cupboards, which it will also make less smelly. It can be used to clean burnt-on stains from the top of a cooker. As we have seen, it might also be used to lift burnt-on stains from a pan, as long as the pan is not made from aluminum.

It will clean and deodorize your wooden chopping board, your stainless-steel sink, and your fridge. You can pat a little onto soft furnishings, and then vacuum it off to clean and deodorize. Being "into" bicarbonate of soda is a sign of knowing your way about the domestic scene. Try to get into the habit of calling it simply "bicarb." Practice rolling up your sleeves while saying, "Soon sort this out with a bit of bicarb."

Other biodegradable, innocent, old-school, Mrs. Beeton-ish cleansing agents include lemon juice and vinegar, or, to put it another way, citric acid and acetic acid. These, too, are degreasers. They can also be used against limescale (see below), and white vinegar in particular is often used, when combined with an equal amount of water, to clean glass (but not frosted glass). When combined with bicarbonate of soda, vinegar will fizz, which can be useful in many ways. You can treat a blocked drain with half a cup of bicarbonate of soda and half a cup of white vinegar, and it's enjoyable in a my-first-chemistry-set sort of way.

White vinegar with nothing added is widely sold as a cleaning agent and is also incorporated into more complicated cleaning products. My wife has a glass-cleaning product that is largely vinegar. I pointed this out to her when she was cleaning our glass-topped table, saying, "You might as well just use plain vinegar; it would be much cheaper and better for the environment." "Your theory is all very well, Andrew," she said, polishing away, "but I've got to get on with it."

Your lemon juice you will obtain from lemons. White vinegar is cheaper than lemon juice, but the objection to using it as a cleaner around the house was neatly put to my by my fastidious friend Helena (of ironing fame), who said, "Do you really want to smell like a pickled onion?"

WHAT'S ALL THIS STUFF ABOUT HARD AND SOFT WATER?

Shortly after my grandfather died at age ninety-six, my father and I were in the backyard of the terrace house in York that he'd owned. A water barrel stood before us, full to the brim and with dust and insects floating on the surface, and my father explained that, in his handsome prime, my grandfather had washed and shaved in rainwater, knowing that while York's tap water was classified as hard, rainwater was *soft* water, and therefore lathered better, and that it was kinder to skin. I remembered then that, even in his shambolic old age, my grandfather had always worn a collar and tie, and that he had been the first person to encourage me to shave.

Leaving aside the science for the moment, let me note first of all that it comes as a relief that both hard and soft water exist in fairly equivalent measure in Britain, determining divergent domestic habits. Our island is increasingly homogenized. If you could somehow replace the high street* of, say, Peterborough with the high street of, say, Doncaster, then some people might notice but not many would object, since they would be interchangeable, having largely the same chain stores. It is also said that our different accents are merging into one: Estuarine English, the whining, cockney tone of London and the Thames Estuary. But in British water, localism is reasserted. York has hard water, as does most of the east of England, including London. Wales, Cornwall, and the far North West are soft-water areas, and the persistence of a shaving lather is one of the things that makes Cornwall feel foreign to the male Londoner, together with the mild climate, the white beaches, and the presence

---

* Our high streets are your main streets.

of occasional palm trees. At first, the readiness of soap to lather seems benign, but you have to work so hard to rinse off that it becomes rather sinister, as does the frothiness of toothpaste when used in conjunction with this water. It makes you feel positively rabid.

But hard water is the troublemaker, and I'm afraid that 85 percent of American water is in this category. It has picked up calcium and magnesium compounds by traveling through soft rocks like chalk and limestone. Water that passes through granite or peaty soils does not pick up these minerals, and so remains soft. I ought to have known that York's water was hard from signs other than that water barrel: by the frosted marks on the bathroom mirror, by the gray fur on the element of the kettle, on the ends of the bath taps, or around the rim of the toilet bowl. This gray, rocky stuff is limescale, as I only recently found out, having previously thought that limescale was perhaps a lime-colored stain made by urine.

I found these deposits disturbing. It was as if everything was being slowly turned to stone and immobilized. The fossilized kettle took longer to boil, and the rubber shower attachment wouldn't come off the bath taps.

In my home today, things are a bit better. Somebody around here must have been monitoring the limescale buildups and dealing with them. But the showerheads are still becoming furred, and I know that the iron—my iron, as I think of it—does not release steam correctly because of calcification.

Water-softening products are available in those parts of the country that need them. But to remove small limescale deposits from bathroom fittings, lemon or white vinegar can be used. Bind the affected area in a vinegar-soaked cloth. Larger areas require a proprietary limescale remover.

Once you notice limescale, you see it everywhere. Look at the grate over the drain next time you're standing at a pub urinal.

8

The Weekly Shop

CORRECT ATTITUDE TOWARD SUPERMARKETS

When I was a boy in Yorkshire, in the early 1970s, I witnessed one of the opening clashes in the war between the supermarkets and the corner shops, which became a war between the supermarkets and the farmers, then between the supermarkets and the environmentalists.

I used to spend the odd weekend at my auntie's house just outside Leeds, and there was a small grocer's shop there run by a feisty man who'd made a name for himself as a top-flight football referee—ever ready to "blow up," send players off, and bemoan the lax standards of the modern game. I'll call him Mr. Thompson. I used to enjoy going into his shop on errands for my auntie because

Mr. Thompson was a very charming, generous, and entertaining man, provided you weren't a longhaired First Division center forward or similar kind of overpaid nancy boy, and his many charitable acts extended to organizing day trips for local pensioners and trying to teach me golf. He knew his customers by name and would talk at length to them, often offering excellent advice, whether solicited or not, while performing a series of actions mesmerizing to my young eyes. He had a stepladder on wheels which he would roll into position when required to fetch something from a high shelf. He would give the merest shove, and it would seem to know exactly where to come to a halt. He then bounded up the steps in one swift movement. I was also fascinated to watch him use the bacon-slicer, which made a singing noise suggestive of lethal sharpness. I always used to step back when Mr. Thompson brought this into play, and I suppose that I was secretly hoping—in my bloodthirsty, eight-year-old way—that he would cut his finger off. The other great attraction was watching him cut cheese, which he did with a wire, like a kind of garrote. Whenever my mother sent me to Thompson's, I would ask her, "Are you sure you don't want any cheese?"

One day I was waiting for Mr. Thompson's rather put-upon assistant to fetch me something like, say, a bottle of lemonade from the intriguingly shadowy back room, when a little old man shuffled into the shop holding a string shopping bag.

"Morning, Mr. Thompson," said the little old man, but Mr. Thompson did not reply. Instead, he stared at the new arrival, and everything went silent and still.

"I saw you going into Vivo yesterday," Mr. Thompson said at length.

Vivo was the shiny new supermarket that had opened a quarter of a mile away. I had heard my auntie mentioning to my uncle that Mr. Thompson had been up in arms about it. So I knew that all the conditions were present for one of his big explosions.

"I only went in there for a loaf of bread and a toilet roll," said the little old man.

A further interval of silence . . . and then Mr Thompson stepped out from behind his counter, which was like seeing a lion escaped from the zoo, and he yanked open the shop door, causing the bell to clatter furiously as he roared, "If you can buy your arse-wipe from bloody Vivo, then you can buy all your other bloody stuff there, now get out and don't bloody well come back."

And so the man shuffled off.

All agreed that Mr. Thompson was a superb grocer, but his shop didn't last long after that. Today, it is a hairdresser's. No small, general-purpose food shop could survive in the shadow of that Vivo, which is now a different brand of supermarket. I, meanwhile, live in Highgate, North London, about five hundred yards from a high street that boasts sixteen estate agents. It is a dead high street, in other words, killed by the big supermarkets, like most of them these days. Once, on a bus rolling slowly along Highgate High Street, I listened to the reminiscences of an old woman on the seat in front: "That used to be the butcher's," she said, pointing to one estate agency, "and that was the *pork* butcher's," she went on, pointing to another. "That was the hardware shop, and that was the fishmonger's. . . ."

Supermarkets are usually located on the edges of towns, thus destroying countryside, fostering car use, and sucking the life out of the high streets. They have Farmer Giles* by the balls and they impose one mood, one tone, one experience where formerly—in the days of small food shops—there had been thousands.

And I am complicit in this undermining in that I have been doing the family shop over the past few months, and I have been doing it in a supermarket.

I tend to perform my ethical acts one at a time (if at all), and to not only take on the weekly shop but also do it in an environmentally friendly way, by using such small food shops as cling onto life in our area . . . that would be too much like hard work. I have considered adopting a solution that could be called pale green: I would buy the boring bulk necessities at the supermarket; I would then buy my meat, most of my veg, and all the finer things in the local small shops. But I can't be bothered to do that, either.

---

* Not a particular individual, readers will be relieved to hear. The term "Farmer Giles" denotes the archetypal farmer.

By taking on the weekly food shop I have made myself heir to a feminist argument in favor of supermarkets, one recently put by Julie Burchill in the *Guardian*: "People who are against Tesco are the sort of people who fifty years ago would have been against labor-saving devices on the grounds that they might conceivably give women time to put their feet up. . . ."

Whereas I know plenty of men who object to supermarkets in theory, I can't bring to mind a woman of my acquaintance who does, and I certainly couldn't imagine any two men holding a conversation of the sort I heard between two women in a charity shop:

"Have you seen the new Tesco's at Colney Hatch?" said the first. "It's absolutely gorgeous."

"I know," said the second. "All bushes and everything—it's lovely."

I was reminded of the time my front right tire went flat very early one morning on a farm track in Devon. I limped into Barnstaple, and called the Automobile Association from the parking lot of the bigger of the two Morrison's supermarkets in that town. As I waited, I watched the staff—mainly women—arrive, and I noticed the way they put off starting work in favor of chatting happily with the first customers, who were also mainly women. It was a lovely, bright morning, and the whole setup seemed a sort of female idyll.

But that article of Burchill's was written to counter an earlier piece by one of our leading supermarket denigrators, who also happens to be a woman: Jeanette

Winterson. After a passage depicting supermarkets as dehumanized and mercenary, she wrote: "This might be because corporate shopping is run by straight white Alpha Males—the world's worst shoppers. . . . They HATE shopping but they run the chains, and behind all the phoney retail smiling and the robotic flat language of fake helpfulness dinned into their low-paid employees, Corporate shopping knows only two words: BUY. GO."

I find myself harried while shopping in the supermarket, not so much by the Alpha Males (from what I've seen of supermarket managers, Gamma double plus would be nearer the mark) as by my impression of being in alien territory. Accordingly, I used to skimp the job; when in the supermarket I was not—to use the language of the sports commentator—"at the races."

I would shop like a man. . . .

CHARACTERISTIC MISTAKES OF THE MALE SHOPPER

I absolutely hated the fact that the word *Hello* was written on the wall of the supermarket, and this seemed to proclaim a sentence of death as I approached the store, and the tethered trolleys.*

---

* Our shopping carts. The word "trolley" is depressing. It evokes a very basic form of transport, and a madman is "off his trolley." We must insert a pound into a mechanism (which is itself often broken) for the privilege of using them.

Owing to extreme incompetence, brought on by a refusal to acknowledge my surroundings, I would sometimes accidentally put the pound coin into the lock on the *second* trolley from the end of the line, so that I would then have to unlock the one at the end as well in order to get it away, which left me with two trolleys, both usually dysfunctional. One might be full of rubbish, and there would be nowhere to put this rubbish, while the other would be splay-legged and listing. Of course, all supermarket trolleys are designed not to go in a straight line, but my two would be particularly wayward.

Taking the least worst one, I would make a sudden charge through the door marked "No Entrance," just because this one was nearer; but I would be penalized by the door automatically closing on me when I was halfway through. Released from the trap by a bemused security guard, I would stagger into the shop, completely mortified by the atmosphere of forceful capitalism combined with female-suburban tweeness. I'd gaze blearily at the magazine racks: *Your Cat, Inside Soap, Let's Get Crafting with . . . Beads!* It was like being trapped in daytime television . . . and all those pictures of Jamie Oliver, who I always think of as having "gone over" to the other side: a man who's thrown in his lot with the supermarket women. Do they like him because he's like a man or because he's like a woman?

I'd look at the depleted bookshelves: books by thriller writers whose names are spelled out in gold lettering, as if that were some guarantee of literary quality; the titles ranked in order of sales, with the mysterious and somehow sinister Rosemary Conley and her bloody Hip and Thigh Diet always in or near the number one spot.*

The whole strip-lit atmosphere promoted anomie. I would listen, dazed, to the colleague announcements. "Would Deborah please come to the checkout?" which always had to end with the formula: "Thank you for shopping at Sainsbury's Muswell Hill," even though the person in question, Deborah, was not shopping at Sainsbury's Muswell Hill but working there, and presumably working very hard—or at least out on a cigarette break—because two minutes later, the announcement would be repeated in a shriller tone: "Would Deborah please come to the checkout, where a customer is waiting. Thank you for shopping at Sainsbury's Muswell Hill."

Morbidly fascinated, I would scan the written notices that dotted the shelves, and which seemed to have been composed by a dead man: "Due to refrigerator breakdown we cannot store any items in this refrigerator. Thank you for shopping at Sainsbury's Muswell Hill." And everything just seemed so flaccid, emasculated: "Mild Cheddar," "Light Bolognese," "Moderate Chardonnay." The fact that there must be people around me perfectly willing to buy a type of beige toilet paper

---

* Rosemary Conley is a British weight-loss guru, infelicitously described on Wikipedia as "one of the big three" in the country. The *Hip and Thigh Diet* and its successor, *Complete Hip and Thigh Diet*, have sold more than 2 million copies.

called "Andrex Warm and Natural" would disturb me disproportionately.

(Of course, nobody *would* ever buy it if you had to nominate products, as in an old-fashioned shop with a craggy, quizzical man like Mr. Thompson behind the counter:

"I'd like some toilet paper as well, please, Mr. Thompson."

"What kind, son?"

"I'll take the, er . . . you know . . . the whatsname . . ."

"Spit it out, lad."

"Well, you know, the, er . . . that top one. The 'Warm and Natural.'"

"Sorry lad, come again. I didn't catch that.")

When I did get properly under way with the actual loading of the trolley, I would come up to the fruit and veg first, because that's what always comes first in a supermarket, the reason being that those shelves are the most frequently replenished. Fruit and veg is near the door for the benefit of the supermarket rather than the customers, in other words, but I hadn't worked this out, so I'd begin by loading my trolley with soft fruits, subsequently piling all the other groceries on top, and I would notice other shoppers—usually women—eyeing my trolley and noting, "He's got a leg of lamb and a bag of muesli pressing down on his packet of raspberries. He must be an imbecile." But it would be somehow even more humiliating to do anything about it.

I would mooch over to the meat counters, vaguely thinking I ought to look out for the special offers. Noticing a packet of pork chops labeled "Two for £4.99," I'd wonder, *Does that mean you have to buy two? If I buy only one, will the checkout person send me back here for another? Or will they simply divide £4.99 by two . . . but you can't divide £4.99 by two. It won't go.*

I would note that other men in the supermarket seemed similarly embarrassed, and that some had tried to abstract themselves by talking into their mobile phones as they moved between the shelves. I would observe the discrepancy between the authoritative tone of their speech into the phone—"I want you to get onto it straight away; copy me in on all the e-mails"—and the contents of the trolley they were pushing: three bags of kitty litter and a box of Cheerios.

My own strategy would be to seek consolation in the purchase of little treats. Having control of the food budget would go to my head, and I'd buy all the food prohibited to me in childhood: miniature chocolate Swiss rolls, Nesquik, a bumper bag of Frazzles. Even as I did this, I would be able to picture my wife pulling these items out of the bags at home and sternly inquiring, "You did remember the garbage bags, I hope?" Not having planned my shopping in advance, I'd be afflicted by a fatal whimsicality. I'd see Camp Coffee and think, *Are they still making that stuff? They had it in the war. It's made from chicory. It's a nice-looking bottle—almost a museum piece. I'll buy some and tell the boys all about it.* Or I'd catch sight of one of those sachets of herbs called bouquet garni and half remember a recipe for stew that involved it. I'd then go looking for the other ingredients, perhaps giving up halfway through, at which point I'd notice that I couldn't fit any more food in my trolley, or that things were starting to fall out of the bloody thing. I'd look at other people's trolleys and see that they were all bigger than mine, and it would dawn on me that I'd taken one of the medium-sized trolleys, one of those designed to be not quite big enough to hold a full weekly shop for a family of four.

I would then approach the checkout, looking for the shortest queue but knowing in advance that whichever one I joined would be held up by someone having selected an exotic vegetable that would not scan, or whose price had never been established in the first place. Or I would be behind one of those slow-paying women, one of those who frowns when told the price, and thinks hard before reaching for her purse. "No, it's not free this week," I would mutter to myself (but half hoping that she would hear). "You *do* have to pay."

As I waited, I would be looking over my groceries. Did I really need that oven-ready Peking duck in a cardboard box? My budget was eighty pounds. I would know I'd overspent, but by how much? When, finally, the cashier began ringing up the total, I might lose my nerve three-quarters of the way through and intervene. "Er, how much does it come to so far?" I'd inquire.

"Eighty-seven pounds," the cashier would say, in a tone made annoying by virtue of being completely neutral. "Is that all right?"

"Yes," I'd say, "that's perfectly fine. I was just, you know, curious . . ." as if it were a matter of purely abstract interest, as if the guessing of the total at a certain mid-point in the remorseless adding-up was a sort of parlor game I liked to play. But what would be the alternative to acquiescence? I could hardly say, "For God's sake, stop now! I can't afford this!"

At the termination of the numb transaction, I would move off with my trolley, now restocked with all the food in environmentally damaging shopping bags. Man-handling my defective trolley toward the exit, I would pass the "Community Notice Board," bitterly reflecting that they wouldn't need to use that word *community* if this really was one: "It's never too late to learn French." "Giggle and Fit—join our classes. You will be fitter, and your baby will be giggling his head off." (I would doubt that, somehow.) "Why not try Shamanic Trance Dance—Trance Dance is a natural way to experience ecstasy and rediscover your roots." "We are researching into the effects of primary lung cancer. If you are suffering from the first stages of lung cancer, please call the number below. A cash fee will be payable."

Incidentally, I was once scornfully surveying one of these supermarket notice boards when I noticed that someone had pinned up a flyer advertising a reading I was giving in a local bookshop, and my attitude changed in a trice: *Very valuable resource, these notice boards*, I started thinking, *the lifeblood of the community*.

A man needs a boost like that as he emerges from the supermarket, because another ordeal lies ahead as he pushes his wavering trolley to his car. In the evenings, gangs of male youths are always to be found loitering outside the entrances of supermarkets. While they clearly think it is very cool to hang about just outside the supermarket, they look with derision on any male who has gone *inside* and actually bought something, and will generally start shouting abuse.

HOW TO BUY

It has come to this: you are doing the weekly shop for yourself and your family. Accept the fact; be in the moment.

Supermarkets boast of the range of choice they offer, but what you want is less choice. Go to a small supermarket rather than a big one. That's why we use Sainsbury's Muswell Hill—it's not too big, and, according to my wife, "the vegetables are great."

Inhibit yourself further by taking a shopping list or a cookbook (see What to Buy). If you shop for specific recipes, you can construct the fantasy that you are the demanding head chef, such a perfectionist that, despite being attended by hordes of assistants, you insist on buying all of the ingredients yourself. You pick up the can of tuna chunks; you scrutinize it carefully: *Mmm . . . dolphin friendly? Check. Best before date? June 2012. Not too much time pressure there*. You shake it, you *listen* to it. . . . Yes, it seems to meet the required standard. You lob it into your shopping trolley. There are other bits of role-playing with which you can distract yourself. A friend of mine told me that when her father—who had been a naval officer—was widowed, he drew up a plan of his local supermarket, noting the arrangement of the groceries so that he would never have to double back on himself while shopping.

You ought to arrive at the supermarket with four or five big reusable shopping bags. If you are still using disposable ones, I have news for you: you are being out-flanked to the left by the *Daily Mail*, which has run a campaign against them.

But disposable bags were socially useful (thanks to the *Daily Mail*, I think we will soon be able to speak of them in the past tense), in that they exempted men from the stigma of buying and carrying shopping bags. In researching her book, *Housewife*, Ann Oakley interviewed forty housewives and found that while their husbands might help with the shopping, they would never carry a shopping bag. They would also push a baby in a stroller, but not in a pram.* I myself will use a shopping bag, but not if it has a flower print on it, or any kind of happy image, or if it's a basket or a string bag, or mounted on wheels. Once,

---

* Short for perambulator; bigger and generally more heavy-duty than a stroller, since the baby lies flat. Any man pushing one is halfway to wearing a dress, or so he thinks.

when our washing machine was broken, one of my sons paid me a pound not to have to take the laundry to the launderette in my wife's shopping bag on wheels. (He and his older brother also once pooled their money to pay me fifty pence in loose change if I would stop wearing sunglasses on the beach at Eastbourne.)

As I mentioned, you will come first to the fruit and vegetables. When you have the choice of buying them loose or packed, buy them loose. I always had a vague idea that fruit and vegetables bought loose in a supermarket were cheaper, but a very game young woman on the checkout at Sainsbury's Muswell Hill once invited me to test it out.

I'd bought three big onions inside a net bag. She scanned them, and the cost was ninety-eight pence.

"How much would these have been loose?" I asked her.

"I should think about fifty pence cheaper," she said. "Tell you what: you're my last customer of the day; do you want to go and get another three onions and find out?"

I fetched another three onions—loose, this time—and she weighed them.

"Forty-eight pence," she said, before archly inquiring, "Which three would you prefer, sir?"

Also remember that the supermarket's own brands will be about 20 percent cheaper. But the buying of "own brand" products seems to import the Orwellian domination of the supermarket into your very kitchen cupboards. And quite often the own brand is pallid compared to the original. I cannot eat muesli except that made by Weetabix (Alpen), or beans and tomato ketchup except by Heinz. There is a lack of glamour about store brands, and I think I once permanently alienated somebody by serving bottles of supermarket white Burgundy at a dinner party. The wine was actually quite good, but I later discovered that my guest was a considerable oenophile, and that he'd brought two bottles of expensive Chablis, which I absentmindedly stowed in the fridge and forgot about immediately after his arrival. I should have noticed a certain tension in his voice as he asked for "a drop more white" with those odd, yearning glances toward the fridge, and the way he fell sulkily silent as I topped him up with more of the supermarket stuff.

Being a man, you are unlikely to find anyone to talk to as you do the shopping, but there *is* intelligent life at the checkouts. Do talk to the people at the registers. I had quite a long conversation with one of them once—all about how Yorkshire, and specifically York, was a much better place to live than London—and, when the red cabbage wouldn't scan, she gave me it for free.

"What the hell, it's Friday," she said, but I knew it was because I'd talked to her.

Do get yourself a supermarket loyalty or membership card. I mean, you might as well. Things go better at the register if you have one. But I had a peculiar experience in this area. . . .

For about three years, I was served in a Tesco that I

frequented by the same young Asian man. He was extremely polite, but rather remote, and had a tendency to say "Good-bye, have a nice day" before I'd left his presence. He always asked whether I had a Tesco Club Card, and I'd either reply simply "No" or, if in a slightly better mood, "Not at the moment," so as to let him down more gently. I might add, "I'm thinking of getting one soon, though," in which case he'd say, "Do you want to take an application form?" But I'd back off from that, saying, "Not just now . . . I might take a form next time, though."

When I began to do more of the shopping, my wife persuaded me to apply for a Club Card. It felt like a capitulation to fill out the application form. It was one thing to be sucked into the vortex of supermarket shopping, quite another to be offered a pat on the head for doing so. It did not seem manly to possess a Club Card, and indeed, on the form alongside "Gender" there was space for not one but *two* letters, as though the answer the Tesco people were looking for was "M/F."

The card arrived, and the next time I went to the shop, the usual young man was at the register.

"Do you have a Tesco Club Card?" he droned.

"Yes!" I said, and smartly handed it over.

There was no reaction whatsoever to the fact that the answer was suddenly different to the one I'd given him about a hundred and fifty times before. He simply swiped the card and handed it back. The peculiar thing occurred when I went back a week later: after totting up the cost of my shopping, the young man simply told me the total. I handed over my debit card, and he didn't ask whether I'd got a Tesco Club Card. I had to actually volunteer the information:

"I've got a Tesco Club Card, you know?"

With expressionless eyes, he put out his hand to receive it, and I had the feeling of having lost a battle, if not a war.

But this all came full circle about a fortnight after that, when he resumed his habit of asking whether I had a Tesco Club Card, and I resumed mine of answering "No" because I found that I couldn't be bothered to take it out of my wallet.

WHAT TO BUY

"What to buy" leads naturally on to "What to cook." You can't do the weekly shop without at least having a hand in the week's cooking. You'd be shopping blind, constantly trying to second-guess the cook of the house. This is not a cookbook, however, partly—but only partly—because I'm not a particularly good cook myself. If I *could* cook, I like to think I'd have the basic decency not to inflict another cookbook on the world. There are far too many of them, blocking out all the literature in the bookshops, blocking out all the light.

It has occurred to me to try and get in on the act, in which case I would do what most other cookbook writers do, namely muster some recipes and project my own feeble personality onto them, with epithets as "This has long been a favorite of mine, and it's just as nice eaten cold the next day!" My selling point would be my own mediocrity as a cook, and my book would be called—outrageously, and yet perfectly accurately—*The Boring Cookbook*. It would include such recipes as "Roast Chicken without a twist" and "Omelets the Andrew Martin Way (Which Is Just the Same as Everyone Else's Way)."

I would thereby join the culinary revolution that has occurred in this country since my dad served corned beef hash every Saturday lunchtime, this being the right, celebratory moment for the most ambitious of the narrow repertoire of dishes he created in a house without garlic, herbs, or olive oil (except for a small dusty bottle, kept in the bathroom). My dad would overboil the vegetables, but his cooking was perfectly all right, especially the corned beef hash, especially if you were hungry. That's how it tends to work with food, I find. You like it if you're hungry. But the modern-day citizen of the Western world, like the snail, moves around on his stomach, and there is an ever-growing industry serving those increasingly rare moments of hunger.

I admit that one consequence of this revolution is that many more men cook today than when my dad was forced to take it up. A celebrity chef is by definition a man, and I have been tempted to make a role model out of one or more of them. *I* could be like Rick Stein, I would think, looking at his winsome, grinning face on the dust jacket of one of his books: amiable, vaguely countrified, and really, really into fish.* But on the whole, I feel defeated and exhausted when I contemplate my shelf full of cookery books. They are a disincentive to cook rather than an inspiration and I suspect that many other men must feel the same. If you know that a man called Antonio Carluccio has written numerous thick books solely concerned with how to cook mushrooms, is that going to make you more or less likely to have a stab at mushrooms on toast?

When I was a boy, we didn't have cookery books in our house, we had "the cookbook." It was a scrapbook into which we pasted the recipes that in those days were printed in the papers as a sort of bonus or afterthought, like nature notes or the weather forecast.

What I am leading up to is the recommendation that the semicompetent cook and shopper ought to arm himself with one or at the most two cookbooks—and then base his whole culinary life on that, or those, book(s). And my recommendation, as a food bible for the plodding generalist, would be *Delia Smith's Complete Cookery Course*, first published in 1978.

---

* Rick Stein is a charming silver-haired Oxford graduate who owns four restaurants in the Cornish village of Padstow. His passion is seafood. He believes that, "Nothing is more exhilarating than fresh fish simply cooked." Nevertheless, he has written eleven seafood cookery books.

I saw Delia Smith on television once, and I was not impressed. "Er, now I think it's time to move on to the potatoes," I seem to recall her saying. But I lived by her *Complete Cookery Course* for the first five years of my married life, in which I gradually took over most of the cooking from my wife.

The book assumes no prior knowledge of cooking and is written in a tone calm and reassuring to the point of inanition.* In the world of the *Complete Cookery Course*, the worst thing that can happen is that a few peppercorns might spill from your pestle and mortar and roll onto the floor when you're trying to crush them. (Delia devotes an entire paragraph to lamenting about, and warning of, this). The recipes always come out right; the ingredients are not exotic, and the end product is reliable comfort food of the sort men and children particularly like. Two pages in my own dog-eared copy are bespattered with, and effectively bookmarked by, spilled food.

The first is the page giving Delia's recipe for Ragu Bolognese. This is the basis for spaghetti Bolognese, lasagne, and other sustaining, Italian-type things. The second filthiest page is that for sausages in red wine, which for

---

* In her public persona, Delia Smith disguises brilliantly the fact that she is actually a very interesting person. She has been a Methodist as well as a member of the Church of England, and is now a Catholic. She has written books about religion and is part owner of a football club (Norwich City). She baked, among many other cakes, the one featured on the cover of the Rolling Stones record *Let It Bleed*.

years was my staple dinner party dish. As a Yorkshireman living in London, this dish seemed to me to strike the right balance between north-country lack of pretension (the sausages) and metropolitan sophistication (the red wine), and everybody always enjoyed it when I cooked it. Or they *said* they did.

Once, a few hours before a dinner party I was due to give, I left my "Delia" on a bus in the middle of London. I flagged down a taxi, and, climbing in, yelled, "Follow that bus!"

"Why?" asked the driver, not moving.

"Because I've left my cookbook on it," I said.

That got him going all right.

"Why didn't you say?" he said, as we roared down the street.

What galvanized him, I think, was the fact that I said "my cookbook," not "one of my cookbooks"; perhaps he was a one-cookbook man himself.

I admit that I was not always faithful to Delia. I two-timed her a bit with Katie Stewart, whose *Short-Cut Cook Book* I found in a cottage we rented for a week in South-wold in Suffolk. This gem of a book, first published in 1967, was lying in a pile with novels of a similar vintage (Len Deighton, Nevil Shute, Desmond Bagley). I believe that this book partly inspired Delia Smith's own most recent volume, *How to Cheat at Cooking*, in that it combines natural ingredients with canned, packaged, or frozen food. For this new book of hers, Delia has completely abandoned her own idiot-friendly persona and gone all racy and decadent. It's as if she's experienced a violent blow to the head, suffering a complete personality change as a result.

How to Cheat at Cooking strikes me as being of no use at all to the inept male, requiring ingredients such as "Seasoned Pioneers Goan Xacuti curry powder" or "sugar snap peas, halved lengthways on the diagonal." (What does that mean?) Katie Stewart's book, by contrast, taught me some useful cookery basics not disclosed by Delia's *Complete Cookery Course*, and here I am referring to that branch of cooking that I think of as "fast frying of thin meat." It was a relief to discover that frying with the gas turned up was a legitimate cookery discipline, since I'd been doing it for years. From Katie Stewart I learned how to cook chops, steaks, scallops, and fillets—and this is really a question of knowing what to dip these things in before frying them. Nigel Slater is also a proponent of the fast-frying of thin meats: chicken fillets with tarragon, cream, and Noilly Prat; lamb chops in vinegar. You're feeling rather peckish now, right? Well, go and buy the books. But three ought to be the absolute maximum. That way you will learn the recipes off by heart, through practiced use of them. You will develop your own variations, and you will be able to visualize the recipes as you navigate the supermarket, which is where we came in. . . .

Allow me to sketch out my own thoughts as I approach the meat counters of the supermarket, mindful of

my favorite cookery writers. As I close in on the meat—
which is the most perilous part of the supermarket for
the inexperienced male, being the most expensive—I am
oscillating between thoughts of Delia and thoughts of
Katie/Nigel.

I will be envisaging perhaps four big evening cooking
sessions a week. To plan for any more would be unrealistic
or just plain depressing. I might opt for two Delias and
two Katies, meaning that I would buy minced beef
and sausages (for Delia's lasagne and beef bourguignon)
and then gammon and liver (for Katie's gammon and
pineapple and liver with aubergines). If this sounds too
bloodthirstily carnivorous, I should say that I might well
stray over to the fish counter, to buy whitefish for Delia's
fish pie, or herrings for Katie's herrings in cider.

My next priority would be to buy things for quicker
main meals: big spuds for baked potatoes, cauliflowers
for cauliflower cheese, eggs for omelets. (Incidentally,
I never waste money on buying big eggs, never having
heard anybody complain, "These eggs are too small.")

I will then try to remember to buy those items my wife
considers "invisible" to men in the supermarket, the boring things: greaseproof paper, garbage bags, dishwashing
liquid. I will also try not to buy those things we've already
got. Once, I came home with six lemons, only to find that
we already had a dozen. That was a depressing moment.
I mean, you only need *two* lemons for a lemon meringue
pie. I once thought of installing a little blackboard in the

kitchen so that I could keep track of shortages. I often see these in kitchens, but they're usually given over to middle-class boasting: "Bubbly for drinks party," "Josh's Grade Eight piano exam, 4 P.M. Tues."

Any man doing the shopping will frequently be reminded by his wife or partner of what to buy and called to account for any omissions. She might wrest the shopping duty back for a while, arguing for example that "We never have enough eggs and milk when you do it." But, being experienced, he will be able to make counteraccusations of his own. "We've no canned tomatoes," he might point out. "I think that if you examine the record, you'll see that we never ran out of canned tomatoes when I was doing the shopping."

The only way to plug all the holes is to shop online, which is very boring.

I SUPPOSE I'VE GOT TO PUT THE FOOD AWAY NOW?

You come home with the food. You drop the bags in a heap just inside the front door. You call out, "I've done the shopping, now you put it away!" and then you stomp off and check your e-mails.

It's a natural reaction to the shame of having spent half an hour in the supermarket. I mean, to all intents and purposes you've just taken a carving knife and cut your balls off. But there are double brownie points for the man who not only does the shopping but also puts it away, which is, in any case, satisfying work. You've stocked up on supplies and you're ready for anything: sudden illness, heavy snow, the withdrawal of your credit card. In the back of my mind, as I pack the shelves of my fridge, I'm Shackleton's quartermaster, stocking the *Endeavour* for its long voyage south.

Rule number one: place raw meat on a low shelf. The biggest faux pas you can commit when loading the fridge is to place raw meat on a high shelf so that it oozes blood onto cooked meat on a lower shelf. Bacteria from the raw meat will breed rapidly on the cooked meat, which is why your fridge should echo the pleasing fastidious-ness of the butcher's shop or deli counter, with raw and cooked meats kept separate.

Look . . . do read the labels. Freeze meat or fish before the use-by date, and freeze and thaw according to the instructions on the packet, and without taking the food out of the packet. (And do not refreeze thawed meat.) It would be terrible to have the verdict returned at the inquest: "Did not read the instructions on the packet." That way your life and death would forever be associated with shopping.

The clock is ticking on all the meat you placed in the fridge rather than the freezer. You've got three or four days to cook that stuff before it self-destructs. But I don't like to freeze meat immediately after bringing it home, because that begs the question: Why did I buy it? The things I put into my freezer are consigned to a frozen limbo and are about as likely to play a useful role at some future date as those rich dead people held in cryonic suspension.

Incidentally, the subject of stocking the fridge requires a brief detour on the matter of fridge management in general. First—to defrost or not to defrost.

Some of you may have occasionally spotted your wives or partners with the fridge switched off, a pool of water rapidly forming on the floor, and all the food that had been inside the fridge stacked on the kitchen table as they hack away at the ice that you probably hadn't noticed forming inside. There might also be bowls of hot water steaming away on the fridge shelves. Perhaps on these occasions, you have been considerate enough to ask what they were doing, in which case you would have been told—if they were still speaking to you—that they were defrosting the fridge. You may have wondered at this. Surely a fridge *ought* to be frosty? The frostier the better, you might have thought. But consider: the more ice there is in your fridge, the less room there is for any actual food.

If you ever did see that shocking sight, it was probably some years back. The good news for men is that most fridges are now self-defrosting. When ice forms on the back or sides of the fridge, a sensor triggers a small rise in temperature, which causes it to melt and run off down a little gutter.

Many freezers are also what is called "frost-free," by virtue of a slightly different system: namely, a fan that blows cold air, which prevents ice from forming. This fan will only work properly if the air is allowed to circulate— in other words, if the freezer is not too full. But if yours is an ordinary freezer, the kind that does need defrosting, then it pays to keep tightly packed with food, since this food will displace the ice that would otherwise accumulate. The upshot, I'm afraid, is that you ought to know which kind of freezer you have. Ask your wife.

You should take the opportunity of stocking the fridge to tidy it up and rationalize it. You might think of cleaning it with bicarbonate of soda diluted in warm water. Avoid using scented detergents in the fridge, since they will taint the food. If you see anything actually moving about inside the fridge, get rid of it immediately. Check the use-by date on that pot of hummus. It's good until the seventeenth, according to the label . . . but of what month?

Purge the shelves of irrelevancies. My own fridge is crowded with whimsical remnants of experimental dishes: a crumpled tube of sun-dried tomato puree, two squares of white cooking chocolate. I toy with the idea of remaking the experimental dish that these ingredients served all over again, just as the genetic engineer John Hammond recreated a dinosaur from a fragment of DNA in *Jurassic Park*, but in the end I chuck them out. If, as the man of the house, you really have taken over the family shopping, and if it turns out that you really do need a dessert-spoonful of red currant jelly not twenty-four hours after you've got rid of half a jar of it simply because you got bored of seeing it in the fridge . . . well, then it's likely no one else will know of your rashness.

Fridges are also colder toward the bottom. It's not so much that coldness falls (I believe) as heat rises. Dairy products should be kept in the coldest parts of a fridge but not near your stocks of bloody, dripping meat. I used to lay newly bought, unopened plastic bottles of milk flat in the fridge, until I noticed that the lids leaked.

Now, cans. . . .

In my boyhood, on the day we took delivery of our first family fridge, my father told me I ought never to keep tinned food in the fridge inside an opened can. The tin, he said, would leak into the food and might poison me. Thirty years later, I shared a flat with a Scotsman called John who said that this was nonsense. I would take the beans out of the can and put them into a plastic container. He would return them to the can, or open a new can and leave some beans in that one, and since we practically lived on baked beans, this became quite fraught.

Well, I can now report that there's the opinion of Scottish John (who was a drug addict) on the one hand, and the opinion of the Britain's Food Standards Agency on the other. It's your call, dear reader. The Food Standards Agency agrees with my dad, and with me; so do the labels on the cans, which usually recommend decanting the contents. The FSA also recommends that fridge foods be kept in sealed bags and containers; that leftovers kept in the fridge be eaten within two days; that you ought to read the instructions on a box of plastic wrap (for God's sake); and that aluminum foil can affect the taste of acidic foods such as rhubarb, cabbage, and many soft fruits.

It is not necessary to put tomatoes in the fridge: they become icy and bland, and Nigella Lawson specifically outlaws it. Tomatoes look nice placed at regular intervals on a shelf, and in summer people will assume fruits so arranged have been grown in your garden. A few crumbs of soil sprinkled nearby will reinforce the impression. If someone asks, "Did you grow those tomatoes in your own garden?" you might try immediately changing the subject rather than lying outright.

Potatoes start growing shoots if kept in a fridge; mushrooms go a bit rubbery, bananas turn black (but I like black bananas), and bread goes stale more quickly because the air is dry inside a fridge. Jam can safely be left outside the fridge. It is, after all, "preserved" . . . but what does this mean? Why is humble, monosyllabic jam so heroically resistant to bacteria? I'm glad you asked me that. It is because the sugar in it soaks up the moisture that bacteria need to survive on. Salt has the same effect. Eggs are considered borderline candidates for refrigeration, but they can harbor salmonella, and what else are you going to put in the egg-shaped containers in the fridge?

Stock and tidy the fridge quickly. Do not leave the fridge door open while you boast to your wife about how you even remembered the toilet roll or while playing about with the Sainsbury's own-brand DVD player you bought on impulse for fifteen pounds, because then the fridge will lose coldness.

Wash all fruit before putting wherever your fruit goes. This is to remove any possible insecticides. A female doctor I know—a cancer specialist—herself got cancer, and when she recovered she said that henceforth she would take two precautions: she would stop smoking (rather fascinatingly, she'd been on a pack a day until then), and she would always wash the fruit she bought.

Rice, pasta, herbs, and spices can of course be kept outside the fridge. These sometimes come in resealable bags . . . which never do reseal, at least not after I've ripped them open.

I decant things into stout glass jars with lids that clamp down tightly. I have learned to decant the food into the jar while it's inside its bag—or accompanied by that part of the packaging that tells me how to cook the stuff, or indeed what it is. Rice per person is easy enough: one cupful of rice, boiled in two cupfuls of water with a teaspoon of salt. But no two recipes for couscous, say, are ever the same.

I once had something in a jar for a couple of years. It looked vaguely leguminous. I would look at it occasionally, taste it (it had no taste), bite it (it could not be bitten), frown over it. I eventually downloaded some food images from the Internet and created a sort of identity parade. It turned out to be pearl barley, for use in thickening soups and stews.

9

"Doing" Christmas

CORRECT ATTITUDE TOWARD CHRISTMAS*

In early December 2005, my wife tripped on our new front doorstep, fell awkwardly, and broke her ankle. Now I am well aware that the word *tragedy* is much overused these days, but this was undoubtedly a tragedy for me, since it meant that I would have to "do" Christmas. This chapter is based on the lessons I learned then. Was the Christmas that I largely managed a Happy Christmas? Well, I've regarded that phrase as an oxymoron throughout my adult life. Sartre said that hell is other people. Christmas

---

* I hope the lessons here will also be good for my readers braced for the sheer joy of Hanukkah or Kwanzaa.

is other people plus housework. It is child care, washing, cleaning, tidying, and cooking with tremendously strong deadline pressure, which is why it merits a chapter here. My friend Roger, who does more about the house than most men, said, "Christmas is like hot air ballooning. When you're up high, and the ground's far off, it's magical, but as you begin to descend you see all these trees, power lines, and house roofs looming up."

And the deadlines are absolute, because Christmas is mostly done in the sacred name of family and children. No man can escape domestic responsibilities at Christmas, as society symbolically asserts with the fact that the pubs close at lunchtime on Christmas Day, while the football matches must wait until Boxing Day. Every man must be a family man then, because the children's sense of wonderment is at stake. If you can't be bothered to put up the paper streamers in the hall, then Christmas this year will not be as magical as it was last year (assuming you could be bothered to do it then), and the children will sense a decline.

The house must also be cleaner, tidier, and more elegant than at any other time in order to impress visitors, whose aesthetic standards are always assumed by one's wife or partner to be of the very highest, however slovenly or unstylish they may appear as individuals. The house is turned completely inside out at Christmas, as exemplified by the way that people keep their curtains open, ostensibly for the public-spirited purpose of showing off the Christmas tree, but also to display the new sofa bought specially to meet the Christmas deadline, or just the pristine state of the room. My own wife spends the whole of Christmas Eve cleaning, while playing Christmas carols very loudly on a portable CD player. It's all "Peace on earth, and mercy mild," but if you get in her way, you're dead. Toward midnight, only one feature of the house is left consciously "distressed": namely the plate, located on the mantelpiece, on which is placed a half-finished glass of sherry, a mince pie with a bite taken out, and a carrot, also half eaten. The original aim was to convince the children that Santa really had paid us a visit, and the victuals are left out today from pure sentiment.

"What's the carrot for?" I once asked, after performing my allotted role of drinking the sherry down to the required level.

"Rudolph," my wife replied, as she swiftly and expertly forged the thank-you note from Santa. "I would have thought that was obvious."

I didn't bother trying to explain that the fantasy did not cohere; that Rudolph, being harnessed to the sleigh, would have been required to wait outside the house (on the roof, in fact) while his boss effected entry. Best to keep quiet. After all, our big Christmas rows—and there's one every year—have arisen from matters almost as whimsical.

In the aftermath of these fights, I have often thought that if Christmas could be somehow reclassified, moved from the category of pleasure and put into that of ordeal, then it might paradoxically be more enjoyable. A man ought to regard it as a test of his resourcefulness, diplomacy, tolerance, and advance planning: as a kind of giant time-and-motion problem, the aim being maximal effectiveness for minimal grief.

I admit that I wasn't conducting "my" Christmas entirely alone. I had my wife around, on crutches, with a notebook in her hand. As the big day approached, she would give me little prompts like "Meat" or "Your uncle Mike's present" or "I assume you've canceled the papers for when we go away." She would remind me of the necessities, and I would address myself to these, but I had made clear that this would be a pared-back, low-budget Christmas. . . .

The trouble with the festival is that, like housework, it is infinitely expandable. In her book, *Martha Stewart's Christmas*, Martha Stewart (who is the *real* domestic goddess) suggests building a Christmas gingerbread mansion with a gold-leaf roof. She herself does this every Christmas: "I don't know what induced me to build gingerbread houses in the first place, nor what inspired me to make them so large and elaborate. Over the years I have made country cottages, town houses—once even a huge baroque church for the family of Ronald Lauder, our ambassador to Austria."

There would be no gingerbread mansions constructed during "my" Christmas—not so much as a gingerbread shed. My observation is that the harder you try at doing Christmas, the greater the chance of rows and disappointments. Christmas enjoyment occurs unexpectedly and accidentally. There's always one day when the weather is Christmassy—most likely the day when everyone goes back to work. But you, by chance, might have deferred your own return to work. You might be out walking on that day; you hear some church bells ringing, a stranger nods as he goes by, and for a few minutes you are genuinely happy. Equally, your best Christmas meal might well be the cheese pastry—bought from a gas station—that you eat on a street corner with your children because your wife or partner has ordered you out of the house as she prepares for the grand dinner party. Or you might find yourself inexplicably happy when she redeems herself by bringing you a cup of tea as you're untangling tree lights.

Christmas pleasure can't be guaranteed or stage-managed. But it is much more likely to occur if you're not exhausted and/or hysterical and if you don't take those injunctions to have a "Happy" one too literally.

HOW MUCH AM I GOING TO HAVE TO SEE OF MY NEAREST AND DEAREST?

If you want to avoid your actual immediate family at Christmas, good luck to you, but I should have thought that the emotional stress of achieving that end would not justify the means. But you will want to minimize your socializing with wider family and friends, because, as previously noted, it equates to housework and is usually no fun at all.

The key consideration is that when, in late November, people begin ringing you up to ask, "What are doing over Christmas?" you must have some sort of an answer. If you abjectly respond, "Well, we've nothing fixed," you'll be at their mercy. Right away they'll be saying things like "Well, are you free on . . . ?" or, in particularly brazen cases, "How would it be if we came 'round on . . . ?"

Get something fixed. Get right out of the country for as long as possible, and take care to label this flight from reality as "a family holiday" in the following sanctimonious terms: "It's been so long since we had a break as a family," "The boys have been working so hard at school," and so on, the idea being to silence any objections that might be raised by clinging acquaintances. If absolutely necessary, you could invite those sorts of people around, on a take-it-or-leave-it basis, to early evening drinks on the day before you go.

I appreciate that most men reading this will not be able to afford to absent themselves for the entire holiday or will not have the nerve to do it. But even a mini-break in Paris, booked for December 27 and 28, can serve your antisocial purposes as follows: one of the people you don't want to see over Christmas rings up with the aim of arranging a get-together. "It would be lovely to see you," you say, and then you leave a pause, letting them think it really would be, before weighing in with your "but": "But we're going away between Christmas and New Year."

They are at a disadvantage immediately. They can see that you have arranged to enjoy yourself over Christmas and that they are not part of the plan. Also, they may assume that when you say, "We are going away between Christmas and New Year" (and you should stick precisely to that phraseology), you mean for the whole of that period, in which case, with luck, you could soon be into "Let's try and hook up some time over Easter, then," or other remote speculations. You put the phone down and nothing's been arranged. Job done.

WHY DO PEOPLE SAY, "IT'S BETTER TO GIVE THAN TO RECEIVE?"

This is professed by many people, genuinely believed by rather fewer. The pleasure of gift giving comes from giving exactly the right thing to exactly the right person at exactly the right time, but this is a rarefied skill, and even those people (in practice always women) blessed with the good taste, willingness to spend time in shops, and background knowledge of another's lifestyle and tastes rarely pull it off. I've seen hundreds of presents given and unwrapped, and yet the number of times I've seen a gift provoke genuine happiness is in single figures. Instead of giving the right thing to the right person, you—as a man—should have a different aim: namely, to give *something* to people who would fall out with you if you didn't give them *anything* and to do it quickly, with as little effort as possible.

I myself have always minimized the labor of present buying, and I started young at this. When I was about eight years old, I gave my father a stone for Christmas. I found it on the ground. I genuinely considered it attractive—it was one of the best stones I'd seen up to that point in my life—but my father did look rather nonplussed when I handed it over. I rallied well, however: "It's a paperweight," I said.

He was very good about it, but then he too practiced minimal gift giving. Sometime after breakfast on Christmas morning, he'd walk up to me, take out his wallet, and hand me a twenty-pound note, saying, instead of "Happy Christmas," "Don't spend it all at once," and this approach must have run in the family, because when my grandfather—my dad's dad—turned up for Christmas lunch, he would open up his wallet and give me a *one*-pound note (exactly the same basic attitude, you see, although in his case unfortunately mired in the monetary values of the 1930s).

A dozen years on, just out of university, I would do all of the shopping for my family in one shop: a pharmacy. Any pharmacy would do, as long as it sold sponges. My stepmother would get a sponge; my father, something to do with shaving or an electrical toothbrush. My sister would get a sponge. It was sponges all around, really, for my women. Natural sponges are considered a luxury item, if only because they're so expensive, and I believe they're easier on the skin than man-made ones. (Well, they'd better be at that price.) The only problem with them as gifts is that, being completely shapeless, they're hard to wrap, or at least hard to wrap decoratively if you're not prepared to give more than a minute to the job.

It's not environmentally sound, but is otherwise a good idea, to buy things in boxes. Looking for last-minute gifts in the off-license—sorry, wine merchants—your question ought not to be about the quality of the vintage but "Does it come in a box?" "Or can it be put into a box?" If you spend more than about ten pounds on a bottle of wine, the merchant can be leaned on to put it in a wooden case, a sort of coffin of its own, which makes it look twice as expensive.

And do always ask about gift wrapping, whatever the shop. It's not necessarily offered up front. You will usually have to pay a couple of pounds for it, but this is money well spent. Remember that a poor present well wrapped is at least the equivalent of a moderate present poorly wrapped.

Be direct with shop assistants. You're never going to see them again. Always ask for a gift receipt. This is a receipt that does not disclose the amount spent (that would be vulgar), but enables the item to be returned and exchanged, at which point the amount you've spent will become apparent, possibly to the mutual excruciation of the shop assistant and the gift recipient. But you, the guilty party, will be miles away.

In 2005, the year in which I did Christmas—my "year of giving dangerously," as I think of it—my wife advised me to buy a box of soaps made by Floris for a female relative. In the Floris shop, the assistant offered me a whole range of soaps including Edwardian Bouquet, Syringa, and China Rose. "Which is cheapest?" I asked, after a moment's thought. It turned out they were all the same price, so I went for China Rose because that was the *nearest* one, and I think I scored a hit with the assistant because as I left the shop, I heard her turn to a colleague and say, "I like it when men do the shopping. They're so much more straightforward."

If you can't decide what to buy any given individual, then consider gift vouchers or certificates. More places sell them than you might think—even garden centers run to them. Old-fashioned ones (at least in Britain) look like Monopoly money: extravagantly plutocratic, with the sum written in large letters. Always ask for the decorative cards that come with them, since they save you the cost of a Christmas card. You then arrange the certificates inside the card, putting the highest denomination one uppermost, but a little askew so that it's obvious that there's another one underneath. The recipient will not dare lift the twenty-pound certificate to see the one-pound one underneath while in your presence. More modern gift cards, by contrast, look like credit cards, and the amount of money you have put on is not disclosed, which is good or bad news according to how mean you are. You are given the choice—torture to any socially sensitive person—of whether to write out that sum on the cardboard that embraces the certificate.

It's a bit of a roller-coaster ride, the giving and receiving of gift certificates. At first, the recipient thinks they're only getting a card. You can see them thinking, *Tightfisted sod*, and then they open the envelope and they're . . . quite pleased. No one's ever ecstatic to receive a gift certificate, but they like them because they lead the mind in the direction of after-Christmas. The recipients picture themselves on their own, liberated from stuffy rooms, family flatulence, and small talk, spending the gift certificate on some book or record of which the giver would probably disapprove (which is the true, unacknowledged appeal of the gift certificate as present).

Always try to visit shops in which you will be able to buy more than one present. Besides pharmacies, this ought to be possible in bookshops, wine merchants, and what used to be called record shops. The wine merchant is a particularly good one-stop shop. Here, you can buy bottles to cover those gifts you can't foresee having to give, which in practice, as my friend Roger's power lines and trees loom, may be more than half the eventual total. (See Do I Have to Buy a Present for My Children's Teachers?) And if you see anything in the shop that you think might be suitable for someone, buy it immediately. Don't think, *Oh, I might come back later for that*, because when you go back it will have gone.

How do you know if you've bought someone the right present?

Well, one thing that the person who's just received something they've always wanted does not say is, "It's just what I always wanted." (If they say that, you can certainly chalk up another missed shot.) Instead, the signs to look out for are a stunned look, a silent staring into the middle distance. These can be mistaken for signs of anxiety, even displeasure, and you might feel compelled to say, "You can change it if you want—I've kept the receipt," or even to apologize for giving it.

Everything sort of goes into reverse when a gift really hits the spot. I've seen it done a couple of times—once when my stepmother bought my wife a small black leather makeup case. My wife went silent and rubbed her eye as though a tear was forming there, and she kept the case in her lap throughout the evening, turning it over in wonderment, and repeatedly muttering, "It's lovely, absolutely lovely . . ." but more to herself than to anyone else. It was a particularly affecting scene. My wife *is* good at giving the right presents, but she had become resigned to never receiving one herself.

WHAT'S THE LEAST AMOUNT OF TIME I CAN SPEND ON WRITING AND SENDING CHRISTMAS CARDS?

I'm itching to write "one hour," but an hour and a half is more realistic. However, this does include the time taken to go to shop, to "choose" the cards (I recommend allowing a maximum of ten seconds for that), bring them home, write them out, and mail them.

How many cards should you send? Well, the average number among Britons is currently seventeen, so that's your benchmark.* The writing out is very quick. Just work through your address book, once again using the criterion: will this person be offended if I don't send one? If in doubt, don't bother. The bottom line is that most people couldn't care less whether you send them a Christmas card or not. It took me years to learn this, and I'd become involved in games of psychological "chicken" (except that they were played only on my side): "Ought I to send X a card? He hasn't been in touch for ages. I'll wait and see whether he sends me one. . . ."

The day of last Christmas mailing arrives, and still no card from X. . . .

"He must have taken against me in a big way. Why? Was it that time that I laughed at his haircut? You can't legislate for spontaneous expression of emotion; he should know that. . . . Anyway, I won't be sending him one ever again."

———————

* Whereas the average American, I'm afraid, sends out twenty-eight.

And then the next day, a card arrives from X: "Sorry not to have been in touch this year. I've been laid low with rather a serious illness, but I'm on the mend now. Drink soon? It'd be great to meet up."

On these occasions, I used to wish that it was legitimate practice to send what might be called a post-Christmas card, expressing the sentiment: "Sorry I couldn't be bothered to send you a Christmas card, but you've been uppermost in my mind all year."

Children's names can be a headache. Strictly speaking, you ought to be logging each new arrival in your address book, but couples who've had an excessive number of children can't blame you for using the time-honored evasion of "To John and Jane and all the family." Better to arouse the suspicion that you can't remember the names of the children than to confirm it by referring to the couple's newly arrived child—actually their fourth daughter, named Denise—as Denis, with the accompanying thumbs up: "Must be a great relief to have a boy at last!"

Incidentally, do not attempt any humorous quips. I had a friend I was sure had been recruited into the security services at university. We exchanged Christmas cards after graduation until I joshingly inquired in one of mine, "How's life in military intelligence?" I never heard from that man again, which made me think I'd hit the nail on the head.

. . .

A NOTE ON HOLIDAY DECORATIONS

While it's all right to drag the Christmas tree behind you as you walk to the recycling center after Christmas gloom, it is not all right to drag it from the garden center into your house at the beginning of the festival. Remember: the run-up to Christmas is a happy time.

Artificial Christmas trees are less work, but, according to my wife, "You have to be careful because a different color's in fashion every year."

"How do you find out which color it is?"

"Go to the Conran Shop."*

A lot of use that is, if you live in Thurso. We always use the same three sets of lights, and one of the most protracted and boring jobs I undertook during "my" Christmas was untangling them after they'd been brought down from the loft. Ever since then I've wrapped them around bits of wood before putting them away. Unless you have good taste, stick to white tree lights—and they ought not to flash. Any decoration involving glitter, cotton to represent snow, or three-dimensional depictions of the Nativity scene is considered appallingly ugly unless it has been made by one of your children, in which case it is a wonderful work of art to be recycled every year.

. . .

---

* The Conran Shop is reliably tasteful, I believe.

DO I HAVE TO GIVE PRESENTS
TO MY CHILDREN'S TEACHERS?

Yes. And here is the Christmas tyranny in microcosm: you must follow the tradition because everybody else follows it. You should buy for the homeroom teacher, and possibly for the headmaster and any specialist teacher that your child might have: for example, in music. The medium of delivery is the actual child.

Newspapers have surveyed teachers about what they like to receive from pupils. Many preferred ethical gifts (addressed below), or said they did, while others favored something homemade by the pupil, including—and here's a glimmer of hope for the tightfisted—a mere greeting card made by the child. Teachers emphatically did not want to receive scented candles, but then who does? In one survey, 15 percent anathematized chocolate ("Last Christmas, I thought my insulin levels had been wrecked forever," said one), while another 15 percent said that chocolate was the present they most liked to receive. It's a question of knowing your teacher. Don't buy ethical presents for unethical teachers, chocolate for diabetics, or wine for alcoholics (although a bottle of wine scores consistently highly among male teachers). The good news is that the practice normally stops at the secondary level. Here, the children don't usually have one teacher for most of their classes, and the teachers prefer to keep the parents at arm's length.

IS IT NECESSARY TO HAVE
AN ETHICAL CHRISTMAS?

It is increasingly expected that there be some ethical element to your Christmas, and the good news is that time and effort can be saved in the process.

Environmental awareness has belatedly brought about the realization that Christmas cards—of which we in the UK send 1.7 billion a year—are a criminal waste of trees. Just think of a Christmas card, with all your weedy felicitations—"Really hope we can meet up in the New Year!"—lying in a landfill for thirty years. If one of your friends brings up the subject of Christmas cards, perhaps in a rather embittered tone, not having received one from you, it is almost possible nowadays to say, "Christmas cards? You don't still send them, do you?"

The alternatives are text cards and e-cards. You can download tasteful free e-cards from, for example, art galleries. But they will usually be accompanied by ads from the organization supplying them. They are in that sense tainted, like the five-pound note given to you by a shopkeeper on which someone has written a mathematical calculation. But people can't really object, since you are behaving morally. You are having your cake and eating it.

One of my friends, who was an environmentalist long before everyone became one, spurns Christmas wrapping paper, which is often not recyclable, and of which we use a great deal. (Never mind wrapping jerseys, I once read that you could wrap the *island* of Jersey in the amount of wrapping paper used in Britain every year.)* Instead, this man wraps his presents in old newspapers. Having spent no money and very little time on the job, he nonetheless asserts his moral superiority over the recipient, who has probably just handed him something conventionally wrapped. He always uses the *Financial Times*, I note, which is somehow doubly intimidating, or perhaps it's just because he knows that anything wrapped in the *Sun* would look like so much fish and chips. He does use sticky tape, and I have just armed myself with the fact that this is not recyclable. I will be pointing that out to him next Christmas. His presents are always generously expensive, I should point out—otherwise, he wouldn't dare use newspaper.

Give abstract, notional gifts like theater tickets. Or practice ethical giving. If you've never heard of ethical giving, you must have instinctively blocked it out because the concept has been promoted vigorously for some years.

Visit a Web site such as www.goodgifts.org. This is a charity working in conjunction with other charities, mainly in the developing world. You might pay thirty-five pounds for a bike for a midwife in Africa, or a shot of bull

---

* Jersey covers an area of 455 square miles. It is the largest of the British Channel Islands. I can find no equivalent land mass that might be wrapped by American gift givers, but according to Earth911.com, as much as half of the 85 million tons of paper products that Americans consume every year goes toward packaging, wrapping, and decorating goods.

semen for the insemination of an African cow, or twenty pounds for a meadow of flowers in Britain. You pay the cost of the gift and a little extra to cover the service. The recipient receives by e-mail or post a card depicting the gift, presumably obliquely in the case of the bull semen. I called Good Gifts and suggested to a spokeswoman that any misanthropic recipients of these presents would not be able to object or appear churlish in any way; that they were in effect trapped. "That's right!" she said, and she cackled, rather.

Buy a Christmas tree with roots, so that you can plant it in the garden for use next year. Or just keep it permanently in the garden. Put some lights on it every Christmas, and when people ask, "Where's your Christmas tree?" point to the window. (And you will not have to sweep up pine needles.)

10

Advanced Housework

EXOTIC CLEANING

Will old wives' tales eventually become old partners' tales? Here, some cleaning theories long propounded by women, and occasionally men, are subjected to scrutiny.

The Theory:

Leave cola in the toilet basin overnight to deal with below-the-water limescale.

In Practice:

I have not been able to test this (a bad start, I know) because we don't have limescale in our lavatory, either above or below the water. My eldest son says he's read on the Internet that cola is sometimes used for cleaning up bloodstains on the road after serious accidents.

The Theory:

Clean black heel marks on wooden floors using a pencil eraser.

In Practice:

This worked, but not as quickly as using an ordinary damp dishcloth. (And then I had to clean up the eraser flakes.)

The Theory:

Clean red wine stains off a carpet with salt and/or white wine.

In Practice:

The more red wine that is drunk, the greater the likelihood that some will be spilled, and this is the carpet stain most feared by those who know about stains and know about carpets.

I remember the parties of my student days. At a certain point, the twin cries of "Oh God, red wine on the carpet!" and "Quick, fetch the salt!" would ring out. Of course, in a student house there may not *be* any salt. "We've got pepper, if that's any good?!"

Sometimes the cry was for white wine, because that's the other traditional remedy, and it might be more easily located. Here's the recommendation of one stain-removal Web page: "If you can bear it (and can afford it!) then pouring white wine onto a red wine stain is actually one of the most effective methods. If you do not want to use white wine or do not have a bottle handy, then salt can be just as effective." But here's Rachel Simhon in *The House-wife's Handbook*: "Do not pour salt onto a red wine stain . . . by the same token, do not put white wine on the stain."

Then *again*, the man who runs my local hardware/ cleaning supplies shop said, "What you put on a red wine stain is *nothing*. Just blot it straightaway with a paper towel. You might get it all up like that. If not, blot with a bit of water. If that doesn't work, you're into your chemicals."

Most of the wine stain pundits conclude, rather ba-thetically, by saying that you clean up any residue with a mild detergent, carpet shampoo, or proprietary wine stain remover. (There's one called Wine Away, which sounds like the prayer of a recovering alcoholic.) But the important question is what to do in the immediate af-termath of the spillage, since everyone agrees you must act fast.

The idea of the salt is that it is supposed to absorb the wine rather than facilitate any chemical stain removal. The argument against salt is that it will merely fix the stain while absorbing some of the wine. The point of the white wine was perhaps nothing more than the assump-tion that white wine is the opposite of red. You'd buy a cat to chase a mouse away. Or it might be to do with its acidic properties, white wine being generally more acidic than red. The argument against white wine is that it does not counteract the red and simply leaves you with a slightly different-colored wine stain.

I asked my wife how she would deal with red wine stains on a carpet. "Well, there are lots of theories, but we don't really have any carpets, do we?" she said, which is true; our floors are mostly wood. I therefore went out and bought a bit of grayish matting and a quarter bottle of South African Shiraz from Tesco ("a soft fruity easy drinking wine with red berry flavours") and poured it all over the mat. . . .

Now the commentators are agreed that the initial spillage can be absorbed by cold water. There is also agreement that you ought to blot and not to scrub or rub. So I blotted; I then tried salt, white wine, and soda water, which is also often recommended. My conclusions were (a) that the man at the hardware shop was right: that you could get a lot of the wine up just by dabbing with a paper towel, and (b) that soda water worked best as the next line of attack.

Obviously, the truly correct and gracious thing to do immediately after someone has spilled red wine in your house is to offer them another glass. No guest ought to be left standing around, holding an empty glass and doing their best to apologize while the host pats away at the carpet on hands and knees, saying over and over again, "Ruined . . . absolutely bloody ruined!"

The Theory:

Clean hard-water stains off a shower screen with white wine.

In Practice:

"I'm going to clean the shower screen with white wine," I announced to my wife. She took this in her stride, merely observing, "You're not using my champagne."

Champagne, I explained, is not technically white wine; in fact, there are more red grapes in it than white. I then reassured her that I had a quarter of a bottle of cheap Sauvignon in the fridge waiting for just such a moment as this. I put a little on a cloth, and it cleaned hard water and soap marks off the shower screen with ease.

But I found the smell of bad wine on a dishcloth uncomfortably reminiscent of much of my early life. As I went over the screen with a dry cloth, it also occurred to me that this process could establish a new low benchmark for wine writers: "A poor vintage, suitable only for cleaning hard-water stains off shower screens."

The Theory:

Remove spilled candle wax from a fabric using a hairdryer and paper towel.

In Practice:

Of all the homespun remedies, this one worked the best. I poured some hot wax on our doormat, then hardened it by pressing an ice cube on it (the wax promptly turned white). I then placed the paper towel over the wax and melted the wax with the hairdryer turned on full heat. I was rewarded by the sight of the wax seeping up into the paper towel in a most satisfying way. When my wife came home, she asked, "Why is this candle on the floor near the door—and these matches?" And then, later, "Who's changed the setting on my hairdryer?" (It was like Goldilocks and the bloody Three Bears.) I explained to her I'd deliberately stained the doormat and then cleaned it up. I pointed to the spot, and there it was: gone.

The Theory:

Eliminate a scratch on glass by polishing with toothpaste.

In Practice:

I tried this first with a large scratch on the underside of our glass table. It didn't work. I tried it on a smaller scratch, and that didn't work, either.

The Theory:

Use a Brazil nut to clean a water mark on a dark wooden surface, or a walnut on a light wooden surface.

In Practice:

"Do we have any water marks on wooden surfaces?" I asked my wife.

"Lots," she replied. "You should know because you made most of them."

"Do you want me to clean them off?"

"All right."

". . . With a Brazil nut?"

She eyed me suspiciously, but gave me the go-ahead to try it on the top of a chest of drawers in one of the boys' rooms. I bit into a Brazil nut and rubbed it over the mark, and it seemed to work. I was basically rubbing the oil of the nut into the mark. I was worried that I was darkening the color of the wood, though, so—having bought a bag of *mixed* nuts—I tried a walnut on another mark, and this too worked in the same way: by not so much removing the marks as obscuring them. I did the work in the evening by the light of a side lamp, and the next day, in the glare of sunlight, I saw that I'd created two dark patches where the water marks had been, so I went over the whole surface with my beeswax polish, with the result that it became stain free and uniform in color. I conclude, therefore, that cleaning with nuts works in the sense that it motivates you to repolish the surface with beeswax.

The same could be said of another piece of cleaning lore, which contends that you can remove water marks with cigarette ash and olive oil. This is a good, fun one to try. You get to smoke in the house, and then to make a sort of mud pie. The ash is to create a mild abrasive, but I found it to be completely overwhelmed by the olive oil when I applied the mixture to a water mark I had made deliberately on the top of an old wooden stool. (And by the way, it is extremely hard to make a water mark when you want to do it.) Essentially, you are oiling the wood and, again, you have to go over the whole surface to conceal the initial cloudy mark.

The Theory:

You can polish shoes with the inside of a banana skin.

In Practice:

This works quite well, so if you're in a hotel (and we're now outside the realms of housework, I admit), and no shoe-cleaning pad or wet wipe is provided, look toward the bowl of complimentary fruit. The trouble is that bits of banana get stuck in the ridges or seams of the shoes. But here's more on shoe cleaning. . . .

HOW TO POLISH SHOES LIKE THEY USED TO IN THE ARMY

In Dr. Caroline Gatrell's book *Hard Labour*, one of the couples interviewed differentiated between "pink jobs" (washing up, doing the laundry, etc.) and "blue jobs" (changing a fuse, putting up a shelf). The man only did the blue jobs, thereby avoiding most of the housework. Most cleaning jobs are pink, or pinkish. Cleaning the car is one exception; cleaning shoes is another, and any man who doesn't even clean his family's shoes is probably thinking of leaving that family.

My father was unusually domesticated even in his youth, and one of the first independent purchases he ever made—at the age of six or seven, in 1935 or so—was a long-handled, double-sided shoe-cleaning brush, which he picked up for next to nothing at a church fete in York. One side was for black, one for brown, or "tan," as he always calls it. Even at that young age, he was convinced that the bristles were of a particularly high quality, and he must have been right, because the brush is still in daily use, and my father has repeatedly promised, or threatened, to bequeath it to his scruffiest grandson.

My father had five siblings, and every Sunday morning he'd prowl the house with this brush asking, "Come on then . . . any more shoes to clean?"

When I was at school, and he was at work, he would clean his and my shoes almost every day, as opposed to the "once a month" frequently, and shockingly, recommended on Internet shoe-cleaning sites today, and if the day was a red-letter one for me—I might have been lined up for some public speaking, an exam, or a school trip—he would cook me a full English breakfast, take my tie, wrap it around his thigh, and create for me a special tie knot: a Windsor knot, which is shaped like an equilateral triangle, and makes almost anyone, even a ten-year-old boy, look like a conservative patrician. He would also polish my shoes particularly vigorously, and even today the sight of my dad cleaning shoes gives me butterflies in my stomach.

I believe that he cleaned—and cleans—shoes for much the same reason that he would do the washing-up: it was legitimized silence, a kind of meditation. He did not want to relinquish the job of family shoe cleaner and therefore never gave me any particular instruction in it. But he did let on that the polish ought to be applied with a cloth and not a brush, and that you ought to rub it in using a circular motion: "Small circles," he would say—it was apparently drilled into him in the army.

Like my father, I am big on cleaning shoes, and in fact *wearing* shoes, by which I mean leather shoes and suede ones, and not trainers.* It's distressing to see any man over thirty in trainers, and the sight of an old man wearing them is tragic. The only thing he's training for is the grave. You can clean trainers by chucking them in the washing machine, and where's the art in that? For instruction in the art of shoe cleaning, I walked into Tricker's in that dandyish enclave, Jermyn Street.

Tricker's is my favorite shoe shop, not that I've ever bought a pair of shoes there—they tend to start at about two hundred and fifty quid for a pair of slippers—but I aspire to. I've always worn the best shoes I could afford,

---

* What you call sneakers.

ever since my first day at university, when I rested my cheaply shod feet next to a one-bar electric fire, and an Old Etonian drawled, "I wouldn't do that if I were you. Your slip-ons'll melt."

If you weren't quite concentrating, you might think, as you entered Tricker's, that you'd wandered into an antiquarian bookshop: dark wood, a beeswax smell, big portrait of the Queen on the wall. And the words "Founded in 1829" are much blazoned about. ("The same year that Robert Peel founded the Metropolitan Police," the assistants like to tell you.)

I collared the assistant manager, Mr. Clive Jones, and began by asking whether a man should use shoe cream or shoe polish.

"I think shoe polish," he said. "Something with a good amount of beeswax in it." He opened a small tin for me. "Here," he said, "take a smell of that." It smelled like a sort of candle factory. "A good shoe polish will polish the shoe and nurture the leather," said Mr. Jones, "and if you want a really high shine, you go for this. . . ." He produced a tin of "Parade Gloss" shoe polish (manufactured by Kiwi).

"I see men coming in here," he said, "ramrod-backed, smartly dressed, and they make straight for this stuff."

"The army types, you mean?"

"Exactly. It's got that little bit more spirit in it for the high shine."

"How should you put it on?"

"With a cloth, and in a circular motion."

"Small circles?" I ventured.

"Small circles," he affirmed with a grin, as though we were two members of a secret society. "That way the polish is really worked in. Then you buff it up with a slightly damp cloth, and finish off with a soft brush."

"What about suede shoes?" I said.

"Bit tricky to clean," he said. "Some people use a wire brush, but I think that's too harsh. The best thing actually is a crepe brush. For more stubborn stains you can use a proprietary cleaner, or a cloth and a drop of washing-up liquid in warm water. But only use the bubbles."

(I knew those bubbles must have some use.)

A few days later, I spoke to a young man—the son of a friend of mine—who's just joined the Territorial Army.* I asked him what his commanding officers had told him about shoe, or boot, cleaning.

"I hope they've given you some Parade Gloss polish," I said.

"Oh, we've got shoe cream in a sort of bottle," he said. "There's a sort of brush at the end, and you put it on with that. It's called an applicator."

An "applicator" indeed. . . . It does make you worried about how we'd fare if invaded.

---

* The volunteer reserve force of the British Army.

MOTHS

A naked man is in bed with another man's wife. They hear a noise beyond the bedroom door.

"It's my husband!" says the wife. "He's come home early. Run into the bathroom."

The naked man does so, an instant before the husband walks into the bedroom. "Hello, darling," says the wife. "Come and join me in bed."

"In a minute, dear," says the husband. "I'm just going into the bathroom." There, the husband sees the naked man reaching about him and clapping his hands together. "What the hell are you doing?" the husband asks.

"Killing moths," the naked man replies. "Your wife complained about them and so I came over. I'm from the council."

"But you're naked!" says the husband, at which the man looks down at himself in apparent astonishment. "The bastards!" he says.

Moths eat clothes. Yes, they're still at it. Unfortunately, they have not been reformed or seen the error of their ways, as I had vaguely thought. Moths in clothes seemed a bugbear of yesteryear, like a fly in the soup or bats in the belfry. But my wife assured me that they were a big problem of today, and that suspicious holes had appeared in some of her own sweaters. She said I should look into moth repellents.

When I went to the hardware shop, the idea that moths

were somehow yesterday's pest was reinforced by the way that the mothballs on sale were in a packet labeled "Traditional Moth Balls." I liked the old-fashioned, no-nonsense label: "For amateur use as a moth repellent." "Amateur use"—that sort of took the pressure off. But it obviously wouldn't do to be too amateurish in using these things: they were not to be used near food or where children could get at them; you were not to smoke when using them; you had to wash your hands immediately afterward, and so on.

As I paid for them, a woman who was buying a dustpan and brush turned to me, saying, "Have you got moths?"

"We might have," I said. "I don't really know—I don't think so."

She eyed my purchase.

"But you've just bought a packet of mothballs," she said.

"Oh," I said, "that's because I'm writing a book about housework for men. Do you have moths?"

"Yes," she said. "I have dozens of them living in my food cupboard."

"I think that's a different kind of moth. Mothballs are for *clothes* moths."

The woman shook her head.

"A moth is a moth," she said . . . wrongly, as it turned out.

Two minutes' research when I returned home re-vealed that this woman had an infestation of pantry moths, which, like weevils, live in dry foods, especially pasta, flour, and rice. (It's no big deal. Sift them out of the food, and then transfer it to the airtight container it should have been in all along.)

Mothballs are designed to deter the clothes moth, or *Tineola bisselliella*, and by the way, if ever someone speaks of "clothes moths" in your presence, do be sure to frown while inquiring, "You mean *Tineola bisselliella*?"

Mothballs are white like mints (take note, fathers of young children) and smell of old country houses or charity shops according to whether you're in a good or bad mood. They contain naphthalene, which can be harmful to humans over a prolonged period, and they can discolor the clothes they are meant to protect if they come into direct contact with them.

You can also buy—considerably more expensively—moth-killer strips, which do not smell. Cedar balls are a gentler and perhaps less effective moth repellent. Cedar oil will kill moths, and cedar scent deters them, which is why expensive wardrobes or chests of drawers are sometimes lined with cedar wood. My wife bought me some cedar balls, having thrown out my naphthalene mothballs before we'd even attempted to use them. (I'd got as far as opening the packet, and she hadn't been able to stand the smell.)

The cedar balls are much better, by which I mean that they smell much better. They are in place among my wife's sweaters, and who knows whether they are doing any good, but our bedroom has the fragrance of a Mediterranean forest. Every six months, you either replace the cedar balls or rub them with sandpaper to restore the fragrance. I'd like to be discovered about the task of sanding down my cedar balls. It seems the ultimate in environmentally sound domestic virtue.

Another mild alternative would be orange peel stuck with cloves. Our youngest son brought us home some bits of decorated orange peel stuck with cloves when he was in grade school. "You've to put it in a clothes drawer," he told us. He didn't know why—he was just repeating what his teacher had told him—and neither did we. I know now that it was intended as a moth repellent.

The larvae of the common clothes moth—it's the larvae that eat the clothes—function as a tax on the rich and well dressed. The little buggers like centrally heated rooms, in which they can eat furs and soft woolens and vintage carpets. They turn their noses up at man-made fibers. The editor of *Vogue* recently came out as having suffered a moth infestation. The moths had eaten some of her Jean Paul Gaultier sweaters, and she wrote a nice rueful piece about it. But if anybody starts actually *boasting* to you about how these epicurean creatures have favored their own wardrobes, you could counter with: "They like it best when the clothes are dirty, you know, and especially if they contain urine and sweat," which is true. However, they will unfortunately settle for perfectly clean clothes as well.

CLEANING WINDOWS

If any part of housework is macho, it's cleaning windows. It has danger to commend it—on average, an impressive ten window cleaners die every year in the UK—and lascivious associations: I'm thinking of George Formby's ode to voyeurism, "When I'm Cleaning Windows," and the slightly smutty British film *Confessions of a Window Cleaner*, starring Robin Askwith. ("Unnervingly mediocre," wrote one critic.)

My ex-friend Scottish John (he of the canned-food fame) used to take LSD, whereas I did not. On the afternoon of a fine day, we were sitting in a pub at a seat next to a window that had just been cleaned. Looking through it, John said, "You know, that's the nearest I can come to explaining an acid trip to you. It's like looking through a perfectly clean window."

I somehow knew what he meant. A scene viewed through a perfectly clean window is more luminous and vibrant than it would have been had the window not been there, which is why most householders do not clean their own windows. They bring in a professional, perhaps quarterly, to do inside and out. Some people see no point in cleaning windows during winter—there's nothing to look at through the windows but darkness and bad weather, and rain is going to fall soon after the job is done, laying dust and dirt on the glass. If there is something vernal, optimistic, and upbeat about the sight of a window cleaner at work—which I think there is—then that's because they're associated with good weather. It would pay any man to study a good window cleaner, and in particular the sinuous descending motion of the squeegee—a rubber blade fitted into a steel holder—which is the key to clean windows.

Our own window cleaner is called Pete, always known as "Pete-the-Window-Cleaner" even though he has many other strings to his bow. My wife gets him 'round about once a month because having clean windows is one of her household priorities or neuroses. She has chosen all of the houses we have lived in on the basis of light, and there's no point having your best rooms facing the right way if the glass is dirty. I began provocatively, by asking Pete, "In what cases would it be appropriate for a man to clean his own windows?"

"If he lives in the country, because there's less dirt in the air outside towns, and so his windows won't need cleaning so often; if he's not scared of heights; if he hasn't got too many windows . . . and if he's broke."

Pete told me how to spot a bad window cleaner: "He'll be wearing a lovely pair of pink Marigold gloves and using a cream window cleaner." Proprietary window cleaners are not required. Windows are cleaned with warm water (easier on the hands than cold) and a squirt of dishwashing liquid. You apply the soapy water with any old rag or, since it covers a wider area, a special applicator, which looks like a laterally extended mop head. The rag or the applicator might look filthy when you pass a window cleaner at work in the street, but that doesn't matter because the skill of window cleaning is in removing the foam that is first applied. For this you use a squeegee, as mentioned. You press down hard with the squeegee and try to do a whole pane in one continuous motion because every time you lift it off and reapply it, you are making another puddle of water and detergent, which will dry as a streak on the glass. You move the squeegee in a zigzag from top to bottom, drawing the froth down with you. If you have left soap streaks, it's better to start the process again rather than try to make piecemeal corrections.

According to Pete, the squeegee revolutionized window cleaning in the 1960s. Before then, a window cleaner would remove the lather with a cloth called a scrim. These are made of muslin and are not as commonly available as they once were. "You know those cloths that you see hanging on a great big carcass in a butcher's shop," said Pete. "It's basically one of those." A scrim is absorbent and has just the right degree of abrasion. Newspaper works almost as well, but you'll put any puffed-up hardware store owner onto the back foot if you walk in and ask for a scrim.

"I POLISH ALL THE WOOD IN THIS PLACE"

"I polish all the wood in this place," you announce to friends, making expansive gestures as you show them about the house. "It keeps me fit, I can tell you, but I just about manage to keep on top of the job." This might earn you some credit as a New Man—at least from anybody who doesn't know that wooden furniture needs polishing no more frequently than about once a year, especially if you've protected it by using coasters and table mats and kept hard, hot, or wet things away from it.

I liked the idea of polishing wood before I ever actually did it, and this stems from my membership of the world's largest private library, the London Library in St. James's Square. I was sitting around with some other members, and we were talking about why we liked the place so much. Was it the fact that you could take ten books out at a time, and keep them for months? Was it the friendliness of the staff? The grand scale of the Victorian lavatories? The views of the chestnut trees in the square beyond?

"For me," said one of us, "it's the fact that it smells of wood polish."

And that was it; he'd put his finger on it.

By wood polish he meant beeswax, which ought to be the main ingredient of the wood polishing product that you employ in your own library, study, or smoking or billiard room. Work it in with the grain using a soft cloth. Leave it to dry, then buff it up. It will fill up cracks and leave a protective sheen, as well as a deep lustrous shine, on the wood (which it will darken slightly).

The more rarefied art of French polishing may be of interest to some readers, if only because the term, written on a card in conjunction with a phone number and placed in the post office windows of our childhood, was euphemistically employed by people prepared to perform fellatio. I didn't know that then, of course. "Seats caned," in the same windows, offered flagellation. I suppose that sort of advertising (and I *will* come to the subject of French polishing in a minute) is all done over the Internet now.

French polishing is the application of shellac to fine antique furniture. Shellac is melted flakes of lac, a resin secreted on trees by a certain species of southeast Asian insect. The idea is to emphasize the beauty of the grain, to give the illusion of looking down into it rather than across it. The application of the polish requires real skill, and most books on ordinary housework either ignore shellac and French polishing entirely, or confine themselves to supplying instructions on how to clean up shellac with methylated spirits when it's been accidentally spilled. You have been warned.

The alternative to polish is oil. This—usually Danish oil—is chiefly used as a sealant on wooden surfaces meant to be water resistant: thus, in the kitchen and bathroom, rather than on the family heirlooms. With furniture oil, you pour it on and then try your best to wipe it all off.

Varnished wooden surfaces take neither polish nor oil and, being very easy to maintain, they are looked down on by furniture snobs. The maintenance of wooden floors is best left to professionals, the consequences of poor finishing being so much more readily apparent.

HOUSEHOLD AESTHETICS: A BRIEF INTRODUCTION FOR THE TASTELESS MAN

As far as my wife is concerned, the major downside of global warming is that low-energy lightbulbs throw an unattractive sort of light.

If she's been away for a while, she'll walk into the house, turn one light on, another off, one up, one down (because she's got lots of them on dimmers), and only then will she say, "Hi." If we rent a cottage for a week, she will appraise the lighting. Some of the table lamps will be stashed in the broom cupboard, others promoted from spare bedroom to living room. There'll be a trip to some local secondhand shops to try and buy some decent lights. Having observed her over the years, I'd say that good lighting was low lighting, but not too low. A good light is like a candle, which never dazzles but never seems dim.

If your own wife or partner is this kind of light-sensitive person, then do replace the forty-watt bulb they inserted with another forty-watt bulb and not a hundred-watt bulb. That forty-watt bulb was in there for a reason. It is in your own interests to do this. Too bright a light makes a middle-aged man look sweatier, balder, and more scrofulous and dandruff ridden than is necessary.

My wife has taught me quite a bit about household aesthetics generally. Early in our marriage, I went to the shop to buy some basic necessities, and I came home with some pale green toilet paper. "Toilet paper," my wife said, as she threw it in the bin, "is white." Tasteful people, it seems to me, wear black clothes and live in white houses. The walls in our house are all white, as are the blinds (we don't have curtains: "they block the light," even when open, apparently); most of our upholstery has white covers, and our lampshades, duvet covers, and pillowcases are all white.

White is not a practical color, but aesthetics trump practicality every time in our bit of North London. What do you suppose would be a good surface for a bathroom or a kitchen? How about something that can't handle water? Something like wood? That's what we have in those rooms, and, if I'm washing up with dripping hands, my wife looks on with eyes half averted, like someone watching a horror film. But wood is fashionable, and that's the important thing.

My art is the fiction that I write. My wife's is her house, which is, unfortunately for her, our house. I do sympathize. I mean to say that if I were trying to write a novel and two young boys and a woman with no particular understanding of or interest in my style were continually meddling with the text, I'd be feeling pretty cross. I would imagine that many men are in a similar position vis-à-vis their wives: they share a living space but exist in a parallel universe. For instance, my wife has put mirrors all around our house. They are not really for looking in but for reflecting light. Similarly, only about two thirds of our chairs are meant for sitting in, and whereas it's all right to look in the mirrors that are not meant for looking in, it is absolutely not okay to sit in the chairs not meant for sitting in. I've been warned that most of them won't take my weight, and I'm not fat. These chairs exist to look pretty, to occupy a space, or to balance another chair, which may or may not be for sitting in. This is my wife's own feng shui. It's not that everything is aligned in order to balance ying and yang; it's more that everything is aligned with *everything else*, so that if I shift a sofa a bit to the left with the result that it is not perceived to be exactly central in the room to someone stepping through the front door, a row can be the result . . . although not so much now as used to be the case. I have learned the ley lines, so to speak, of the house, and give them due reverence. And if I should forget, I have a refresher course when we have guests, and the look of the house is optimized. The house is, as my wife calls it, styled.

This is not just a matter of cleaning and tidying. The aim is to indicate a certain lifestyle, and a very rarefied one at that. It's instructive to look at the kinds of publications allowed to be left lying around: *Vogue*, *Wallpaper*, *World of Interiors* (my wife is very unusual, in that she actually reads *World of Interiors* rather than just looking at the pictures). My own weekly magazine, *Autosport*, is immediately hidden away never—quite often—to reappear. Somebody in our house, the visitor is invited to notice, is halfway through a leather-bound copy of *Nicholas Nickleby*, whereas someone else—a child, presumably—is in the middle of a rather nice edition of *Five Children and It* by E. Nesbit. It's a sort of higher tidying. But I like the house when it's been styled, and it's sometimes the most pleasurable aspect of our socializing.

11

Some Psychological Aspects of Men's Housework

THE IMPORTANCE OF FOLLOW-THROUGH

In her book *Hard Labour*, Dr. Gatrell quotes a man—a scientist—who, when his wife suggests that he might like to clean the bath, answers, "I'll do it, but I won't do it *then*. I'll do it when I've got a free slot." Another of her interview subjects will "do" birthdays, but only those of immediate family members. He won't send cards to more distant relatives or mere friends.

Both of these men, it seems to me, lack the ability to follow through. The first man gets out of the bath and thinks that's the end of the process, whereas a more domesticated man, or most women, will not consider the process of bathing to have ended until he or she has cleaned the bath. The second man accepts that some people do have birthdays, and that something needs to be done about it. But again, the guillotine comes down: "I'll send a card or buy a present for my father, but not for the long-standing friend of the family."

Let's take dinner parties. For most men the guillotine falls when the dinner party ends and he and his wife say good night to the hostess with a kiss on the cheek. "Lovely meal," they might remember to say, and that's it, whereas the event is still ongoing for that man's wife or partner, because there is . . . well, let's see if any of my male readers can guess. . . .

That's right: there is the *thank-you note* to be written. Looking at one we'd received once (it was signed "Jane"), my wife said, in a tone poised very finely between amusement and regret, "You know, we've never received a thank-you note from the male half of a couple. . . . Some things never change."

Or let's go back to lightbulbs.

As you walk around your house or flat, you'll notice that some lights, when switched on, do not come on. This is invariably because the bulb has gone. What do you do? You go first into a state of denial, repeatedly trying the switch. You then switch on the next-nearest light and mention to your partner at about midnight, just before you both go off to sleep, "The bulb's gone in the side light in the end room," as if there were some virtue in having noticed the fact even if you didn't do anything about it.

If you'd followed through, you would have changed the bulb straightaway.

Since you're going to be mooching about the house anyway, you might as well incorporate into that mooching a steady, ruminative tidying and sorting-out. It ought to be a flow rather than a staccato rhythm. Refute the truism contained in the following well-known joke: "Q: How many men does it take to change a toilet roll? A: Nobody knows—it's never been done."

The shame in not changing the toilet roll does not come from the omission so much as from hoping that everybody will think you didn't notice that it needed changing. Which man hasn't at some point entered a bathroom, perhaps with the idea of cleaning his teeth or applying deodorant, only to abandon the plan and dart from the room in panic on seeing that the toilet roll needs changing? Yes, it is a very irksome job. You have to remove the empty roll, throw it away or recycle it, and then locate the stock of new toilet rolls. You have to put the new one in place, and unpick the end of it so as to get it started. No wonder it's so hard to resist drawing attention to the fact of your having done the job: "I don't suppose," you announce, as you sit down to lunch with your family, "that anyone's noticed the new toilet roll in the bathroom?"

Let's assume you are sufficiently domesticated to throw what is obviously rubbish into what is obviously the bin. But how often do you take the garbage bag out of the kitchen bin, tie a knot in the top, chuck it outside, sprinkle bicarb into the empty kitchen bin (so as to neutralize odors), before reinserting a fresh bag? A kitchen bin is both a convenience—for obvious reasons—and an inconvenience in that it must occasionally be emptied, which requires work. It is more convenient than it is inconvenient, and the inconvenience is the price you pay for the convenience. The bin must be seen holistically, as they say in Crouch End, London N8.*

To see the kitchen bin in this way requires a qualitative change. It will dictate that you don't just empty the kitchen bin occasionally but every single time you see it full. That's how you'll know that you've made the shift.

IS HOUSEWORK THERAPEUTIC?

For a few years, it was thought that moderate physical activity, including things such as walking to the shops, ironing, and making the bed, might bring some of the psychological and physical benefits associated with more vigorous exercise. But this slob's charter now appears to have been revoked: for exercise to be useful, you ought to be out of breath.

There are periodic attempts in the women's pages of the papers to reinstate housework as beneficial exercise.

---

* An area of stolid, redbrick Victorian housing upon which the residents have imposed a sort of Greenwich Village fantasy of liberal bohemianism.

The *Sun* recently ran an article headlined "Tone up with Housework-out." "Daily dishes," I read, "are a great opportunity to stretch side and back muscles. As you take dishes out of the dishwasher, turn your body from side to side, allowing your hips and torso to twist while you reach to put the clean dishes away on high and low shelves." That exercise was called "Unload and Lift." Another one—particularly well named, I thought—was called "Laundry Toss": "Stand about ten to fifteen feet away from the washing machine. Hold the dirty laundry basket about waist height on your left side. . . ."

But for all the feebleness of the case for housework as exercise, plenty of men have told me they find housework therapeutic, and I know why.

By profession I am a writer, which means I spend much of my day avoiding writing. I'm not necessarily doing nothing in that time. Instead, I am engaging in what the psychologists call "displacement activities." For some writers, these involve cutting their fingernails; putting their books in alphabetical order; looking themselves up on the Internet; writing letters of complaint to neighbors about the barking of dogs, the screaming of children, the swearing of builders, and so forth. All of these are useless neurotic activities, whereas it is open to the writer or other "creative" people working from home to incorporate housework into his displacement activities.

Anyone who does an intellectual job whether from home or in an office or both would benefit from doing some physical labor not requiring concentrated thought. The boringness of housework—which arises from its lack of intellectual content, which in turn has driven generations of women half mad—is thus turned to advantage. The point is that you can think of other things while doing housework. The moral law dictating that a watched pot never boils also dictates that inspiration—as we writers call any idea at all about what to do next—doesn't arrive when consciously striven for. Instead, it comes when you're applying candle wax to the runner of a wooden drawer to make it slide better. And if it doesn't come then, at least you've got a smoother-running drawer.

I always look for the counterweight of physical activity in the lives of successful, cerebral men, and I usually find it: Dickens walked an average of about ten miles a day; Gladstone chopped down trees while Disraeli planted them; Martin Amis plays tennis in the afternoon. But it's not a matter of keeping fit, I think, so much as finding activities that offer a known beginning, a known end, and a finite duration. This is partly the appeal of tidying up and having a "clear-out," the psychological benefits of which are self-explanatory . . . although this has not prevented the growth of an industry that explains them. Decluttering is, according to the Association of Professional Declutterers and Organisers, "an exciting new service industry" in the UK, whereas "our colleagues in the USA and Canada have been supplying decluttering services for many years."

I have a special bin in the garden for all materials other than regular rubbish and recycling. Every couple of weeks I take this to the municipal dump along with as many other household goods as possible. I so enjoy this regular purgation that, if I'm feeling at all depressed on a weekend, my wife might tentatively suggest, "Why don't you go to the dump, Andrew?"

"There's nothing to take," I'll reply gloomily.

"Well, you've got all the stuff in your special bin, and I'm sure there's a few other bits and pieces."

I'll brighten at that, possibly suggesting, "I know, I'll take the lawnmower."

"Wait a minute. . . . Why? Is there anything wrong with the lawnmower?"

"It's too . . . it's a bit too small. I'm thinking of getting another one anyway."

HOW MUCH DO WOMEN KNOW ABOUT HOUSEWORK?

Some men might be deterred from taking on more housework by the thought that too much specialist knowledge is required, that the learning curve is too steep. They might be further intimidated by the thought that women know all about this subject, that they will never catch up with the women. I used to feel this, but I was heartened by my early questioning of my wife.

"How long has Toilet Duck been on the market?"*

"No idea."

"Is bleach biodegradable?"

"Could be. Look it up on the Internet."

"On a steam iron, why is there a switch that allows you to turn the steam off? When would you need to use that?"

"What switch?"

"Why is dishwasher salt called 'granular'? Surely *all* salt is granular?"

"I don't know, Andrew, I just don't know."

I would say that most women know more about housework than most men, but I wouldn't put it much higher than that. There's a huge variation from woman to woman. After I'd started writing this book, I would test them out at parties:

"How would you disinfect a wooden chopping board?" I would ask some new female acquaintance.

"Scrub it with salt."

"Good. Why?"

But they probably wouldn't know why. They'd just vaguely heard that salt was the thing to use. They might not know how to clean a chopping board at all; some might be interested to find out; others wouldn't care, and

---

* Toilet Duck is a toilet cleaner in an odd-shaped bottle. The angled neck, which is "designed to reach right under the rim," is billed as "unique," and tends to stick in the mind. It used to be quite widely available in the United States – less so now, I believe.

would be defiant about it: "I've never disinfected the flaming chopping board, and do you know what? My children have hardly had a day's illness in their lives." And that's all very healthy, because perfectionism in housework can easily lead to neurosis.

In the course of writing and researching the book, I myself began to develop a condition that might be regarded as the psychological equivalent of housemaid's knee: housemaid's eye. I would see the world through the eyes of the domestic operative. As I traveled about the country, I noted the way the products for dealing with limescale came and went according to the hardness or softness of the water in that area. Visiting a friend's house, I might furtively jab my hand down the back of the sofa, encountering a mass of grit. *Mmm . . . somebody needs to get busy with the crevice tool*, I'd think. And I would hesitate before making statements of a sort I'd once have bandied about quite readily: things like "Let's light the fire," "Why don't we have a dinner party?" or "No, don't worry about taking your shoes off." Because I was now able to envisage the amount of work involved. On the other hand, I still do stub my cigars out in our best china cups, and I'm not always as scrupulous about . . . well, never mind. The point is that I think that obsessive-compulsive disorder is some way off yet.

The slogan of *The Best Way Cook Book*, "written by housewives for housewives" and a bestseller of 1909, was "There is a right way and a wrong way of doing everything. There is also a best way." For much of the twentieth century, housewives, as they were then commonly called, were encouraged to learn the best way. The justification of their existence was that they were good about the house. Fewer women think like that today, and so the notion of housework has changed: it is an acknowledged chore, to be got out of the way as quickly as possible. Working women scramble through it, and men should think the same. Don't worry about the best way; just do *something*, for God's sake.

HOW CAN I MAKE MY SONS DO HOUSEWORK?

My sons recently came into my study and asked whether they could make toasted sandwiches for themselves and their friend who was over for the day. They offered me one, but I'd already eaten.

I was vaguely aware, from noises off, of the toasted sandwiches being made (the usual whooping, jeering, cackling, and screaming), and then of the boys going outside to play football.

Here is what I found when I walked into the kitchen: Next to the sink, half an onion was loosely wrapped in a dishcloth. A packet of ham stood open on the work surface next to the sink, and one slice of ham was on the floor directly below. On the window ledge behind the sink was a carton of orange juice standing in a pool of orange juice. A quantity of dirty crockery had been heaped into the sink, and there was more in the dishwasher, which stood gaping open. A good deal of dirty cutlery was scattered generally about, including a pair of salad servers even though there was no evidence of any salad having been prepared. Next to the bread bin was the flashlight, normally kept in the cupboard under the sink. (This was lunchtime, and on a very bright day.) At first, I couldn't see the sandwich maker, but then I spotted it on a chair, and for a moment I thought it had been split clean in two, but it turned out that only one of the two hinges had come away, and I was able to click it back into position.

I went outside and called my sons into the kitchen. We surveyed the scene. After a period of pretending not to know what I meant (*"What?"* the boys kept saying. *"What do you want to see us about?"*), they became aggrieved: "It's the last time we offer to make you a sandwich," etcetera. Probably I had chosen the wrong moment, but it was disturbing to think that, if they could leave the kitchen in that state while feeling well disposed toward me, what might they be capable of when not acting in a spirit of domesticated goodwill?

Their negligence of tidiness and hygiene is often staggering. If they've spent a few hours lounging about on a sofa, I'll find not just loose change and candy wrappers down the back but—for example—whole empty yogurt containers; single socks; broken mobile phones; and little springs, circuit boards, and other pieces of hardware that turn out to be the constituent parts of the TV remote.

In *Hard Labour*, some of Dr. Gatrell's male interviewees had become diligent about housework in reaction to their fathers, who had been the opposite. My own father was apparently like that, and from an early age. Having noted that his mother (who died before I was born) was "absolutely knackered" on Mondays, these being wash-days, and having also observed that his father gave her no help whatsoever about the house, he would rush home from school on Mondays to wind the hand mangle for her. He continued to do this throughout his teens, and in return his mother never complained when he went out underage drinking or, his particular vice, gambling at the racecourses of northern England.

I emulated his domesticated habits, but I sometimes think that my sons have rebelled against my own domesticity, which increases my annoyance, because I am being penalized for having done the right thing.

It's not that they're entirely dissolute. Both have household jobs they've taken to and will carry out with little persuasion. The youngest likes mopping the bathroom floor ("Squirty stuff, you know . . . it's fun"); the oldest quite enjoys cooking. Both will occasionally undertake, without any prompting, a purgatorial tidying of their bedrooms, especially the younger boy, so that things are left not just tidied but thoroughly rationalized, and my wife will come up to me, awestruck, and say, "Isn't it amazing what a good night's sleep will do for him?"

Both are well organized in the areas of life they think are important, which so far includes schoolwork. We do push them hard about schoolwork, and I think they've decided that trying hard at it is their main obligation. Any housework they undertake is a favor to their parents, and especially to their mother.

Their line is that they would do much more about the house for me if I "didn't shout at them all the time," if I asked nicely. And I have noticed that a moderated tone of voice can work. If I were able to say, in an easygoing tone, "Would you mind seeing if you can round up the parts of the TV control and fit it together so that I can watch my film tonight?" then it might pay dividends, or "Oh, by the way, would you mind taking the remains of your dinner out from underneath the sofa if it's not too much trouble?" I sometimes try to put my requests as a neutral drone: "Bathwater out . . . clothes in washing basket . . . towel on towel rail . . . take blazer off floor . . . hang blazer up." But this winds them up just as surely, and one of them will eventually snap: "What's your *problem*?"

Maybe I should be more grateful when they do pull their weight. This is the line advocated by the authors of *The Happy Home*, a domestic guide published in the mid-1950s by The Good Housekeeping Institute, and I like the innocence of health and safety in the example given: "A hearty 'Thank you for chopping the wood. That will be a real help to me' creates in the child a readiness for further co-operation."

I admit that I only really bug my children about doing housework when I'm in a bad mood myself about something else entirely. Usually, I'm happy to tidy up after the boys. It gives me a sense of superiority over them to unknot their shoelaces or dust the covers of their lamentably undisturbed dictionaries, and part of me subscribes to their slobbishness—I see something noble in it.

In atavistic moments, I do not think it is the destiny of any man to have to do housework. I do not imagine that Mick Jagger—to take the preeminent Alpha Male of our times—does very much of it. Unfortunately, I haven't managed to dodge it in my own life, but perhaps my sons will succeed where I failed. Perhaps they, like Sir Mick (resident, at the time of writing, in one of the West End's better hotels), will be able to throw money at the problem.

Which brings me to . . .

CONCLUSION

The Coward's Way Out

I picture the male reader finishing this book in disgust and flinging it toward the trash or—a vision only marginally less displeasing—into the recycling crate. "Screw that," he says. "We're getting a cleaner."

Middle-class prosperity, the increasing willingness of women to go out to work, the collapse of the manufacturing industry, and the influx of migrant labor combine so that one in ten households now employs some form of domestic help.

Many men would consider themselves virtuous for removing the domestic burden from the woman in their lives and putting it onto another woman. In fact, the feminists themselves are divided on the issue, and let's not forget that some professional cleaners are men, especially those who come from agencies. Going through an agency is the most expensive way of hiring a cleaner. The best way is on the recommendation of a friend. A riskier way is to look in any post office window:

"Cleaner. Honest, mature, full-time drive license. Speaks many language."

"Polish girl is looking for housework. This is one of my references from great people I work for: 'This young lady is trustworthy, loyal, honest, keen to please, and can balance many varied activities.'"

"Hi! My name is Kamila and I am looking for job in cleaning. I am friendly, responsable and a patience person." (Kamila must mean "patient," but is patience necessarily a virtue in cleaning?)

We in our house have employed various weekly cleaners at various times. They've been women exclusively, and I've liked them all. None has affected me like Mrs. Buffard, but they all hang up the dishcloth between the taps as she did—the universal sign of a good cleaner.

A cleaner enforces a code of civility in the house. You're much less likely to start screaming at your loved ones if there are third parties around. But they can create work in that of course you have to clean the whole house before they come around (my wife always does this); you might also feel the need to help with their emotional lives (my wife always does this as well). You might labor to maintain the standards they've set after they've gone. They will also present you with shopping lists of recondite items so as to prove they know their job: descalant for the iron, antimildew stuff for the shower curtain, and so on. And they get in your bloody way. You dash into the bathroom, bursting for a slash, and that's when they're putting the blue stuff in the toilet bowl. You want to cross the hall in your muddy boots? That's when they're mopping the hall.

Cleaners in London charge anything between about eight and twenty pounds an hour, which is why, for all the popularity of hiring a cleaner, you don't very often hear of anyone having "a daily woman" anymore, and hiring a once-weekly cleaner will, I'm afraid, not obviate the necessity of reading this book. (I am now addressing those men who have chosen to start with the conclusion.)

Ironing is usually dealt with by separate negotiation and charged at a lower rate in recognition, perhaps, of the enjoyable nature of ironing. I wasn't entirely lying when I wrote at the outset that I enjoyed the job. But sometimes, when I've not kept up with it, I have the illusion of all the unironed clothes—and the laundry in general—chasing me, as Michael Hordean is chased along a bleak seafront by a ghostly, sheetlike thing in Jonathan Miller's adaptation of the M. R. James story, "O Whistle and I'll Come to You."

This is the way of it with all housework. It just keeps on coming. Most men, I know, try to wish it away. In their heads they are Mick Jagger, and if *you* are one of those, then I say go into the bathroom and look in the mirror. What do you reckon? Still in with a chance? Either way, when you've finished staring into the mirror, look *at* the mirror.

Isn't that a hard-water mark?

CONCLUSION

ACKNOWLEDGMENTS

Aside from the person mentioned in the dedication, I am grateful, in no particular order, to the following: Colin Hasson, press officer and lifetime vice president of the British Institute of Cleaning Science; Henry the Mattress Doctor; Dr. Val Curtis of the Hygiene Centre at the London School of Hygiene and Tropical Medicine; Fiona Freedman; Sandra (among others) at John Lewis; Maggie Wood at the Museum of Domestic Design and Architecture at Middlesex University; Brian of G and S Group Service; Dr. Caroline Gatrell of Lancaster University . . . and to Anne, the woman who has washed more than 120,000 socks.

ABOUT THE AUTHOR

Andrew Martin trained as an attorney before becoming a journalist and novelist. A regular contributor to the *Guardian*, he has also written for the *Daily* and *Sunday Telegraph*, the *Independent*, and *Granta*, among many other publications. His seven novels include five titles—beginning with *The Necropolis Railway*—featuring the young Edwardian detective Jim Stringer. He has also written short stories and radio plays. He lives with his wife and two children in London.